westermann

W0465198

CAMDEN MARKET

6

Arbeitsbuch Inklusion

CAMDEN MARKET 6

Arbeitsbuch Inklusion

Autorin: Christina Wolkenhauer (Rosenow)
Unter Mitwirkung von: Henriette Vahle und Daniel Walker
Fachliche Beratung: Sandra Schünemann und Miriam Skott

Zusatzmaterialien zu Camden Market 6

Materialien für Lehrerinnen und Lehrer

- Textbook für Lehrkräfte 6 (ISBN 978-3-14-149130-2)
- Materialien für Lehrkräfte 6 (ISBN 978-3-14-149131-9)
- Differenzierende Kopiervorlagen 6 (ISBN 978-3-14-149136-4)
- Lernerfolgskontrollen 6 (ISBN 978-3-14-149133-3)
- CD für Lehrkräfte 6 (ISBN 978-3-14-149134-0)
- DVD für Lehrkräfte 6 (ISBN 978-3-14-149135-7)
- BiBox für Lehrer/-innen (Einzellizenz) (WEB-14-149137)
- BiBox für Lehrer/-innen (Kollegiumslizenz) (WEB-14-149091)
- Online-Diagnose zu Camden Market 6 www.onlinediagnose.de
- kapiert.de zu Camden Market 6 www.kapiert.de/schule

www.westermann.de/camden-market

Materialien für Schülerinnen und Schüler

- Textbook 6 (ISBN 978-3-14-149119-7)
- Textbook 6 (Softcover) (ISBN 978-3-14-149214-9)
- Workbook 6 (ISBN 978-3-14-149120-3)
- Interaktive Übungen 6 (ISBN 978-3-14-149367-2)
- Klassenarbeitstrainer 6 (ISBN 978-3-14-149123-4)
- Grammatiktrainer 6 (ISBN 978-3-14-149124-1)
- Wortschatztrainer 6 (ISBN 978-3-14-149391-7)
- Vokabelbox 6 (ISBN 978-3-14-149125-8)
- Let's talk 6 (ISBN 978-3-14-149401-3)
- Let's write 6 (ISBN 978-3-14-149127-2)
- Zoom-App zu Camden Market 6 www.zoom-app.de
- Westermann Vokabeltrainer-App zu Camden Market 6 www.westermann.de/vokabeltrainer
- BiBox (Einzellizenz für 1 Schuljahr) (WEB-14-149128)
- BiBox (Einzellizenz für 4 Schuljahre) (WEB-14-103364)
- BiBox (Einzellizenz PrintPlus für 1 Schuljahr) (WEB-14-149129)

westermann GRUPPE

Druck A[1] / Jahr 2021
Alle Drucke der Serie A sind im Unterricht parallel verwendbar.

Redaktion: Henriette Vahle und Daniel Walker
Vokabelanhang: Lisa Hambrecht, Köln
Illustrationen: Ulf Marckwort, Kassel
Umschlaggestaltung: LIO Design GmbH, Braunschweig
Layout: JANSSEN KAHLERT Design & Kommunikation GmbH, Hannover
Druck und Bindung: Westermann Druck GmbH, Braunschweig

ISBN 978-3-14-**149122**-7

Welcome back to Camden Market!

Megan McGregor

I'm twelve years old.
I have got a half brother, Fergus.
I have got a dog, Sir Barks-A-Lot.
I like rugby and animals.

I'm twelve years old.
My parents have got a shop.
I have got a sister, Neela, and a brother, Pradeep.
I like music and football.

Sandeep Chopra

Jasmine Bolt

I'm twelve years old.
I have got a brother, Jason.
I have got a cat, Bagheera.
I like basketball and taking photos.

I'm thirteen years old.
I have got two sisters, Sarah and Emma, and a brother, Steven.
I have got two budgies, A and B.
I like drawing and computers.

Ben Hancock

Symbole und Verweise

Diese Dinge übst du:

Hören   Sprechen   Lesen   Schreiben

Hier gibst du Informationen aus einem englischen Text auf Deutsch weiter.

4 Diesen Text kannst du dir anhören. Die Hörtexte werden online angeboten. Gib den Webcode **WES-149122-001** auf www.westermann.de/webcode ein.

Wörter in blauer Schrift kannst du in deinen eigenen Sätzen austauschen.

Diese Kästchen werden dir im Buch begegnen:

Hier erfährst du interessante Dinge über Großbritannien.

Hier findest du Tipps zu den Aufgaben.

Hier findest du wichtige Redemittel.

Theme 1

After the holidays

In diesem *Theme* beschäftigst du dich mit ...

- deinen Ferien und den Ferien anderer,
- den Landesteilen Großbritanniens,
- Unterschieden und Gemeinsamkeiten von britischen und deutschen Schulen,
- deiner Schule.

1 Megan's holidays

a) Look at the pictures. Say what you can see.
Sieh dir die Bilder an. Sag, was du sehen kannst.

I can see ...

b) Listen to Megan and number the pictures. 1
Höre Megan zu und nummeriere die Bilder.

c) Read the sentences and match them with Megan's photos.
Lies die Sätze und ordne sie Megans Fotos zu.

☐ I played with my little half brother Fergus.

☐ On sunny days I met my friends in the park.

☐ I went to Spain with my mum and we stayed in a hotel.

☐ I visited my dad in Edinburgh and we went to the castle.

2 My holidays

Talk about your holidays with a partner.
Sprecht zu zweit über eure Ferien.

My holidays were ...

My holidays were great.

funny | boring | interesting | exciting | ...

I was in England.

in Spain | at my grandparents' | in Turkey | at the lake | at home | ...

The weather was good.

bad | warm | rainy | hot | cold | windy | ...

I went to the zoo.

played football | met my friends | watched ... | visited ... | ...

3 Back home

a) Look at the title. What does it mean in German?
Sieh dir die Überschrift an. Was bedeutet sie auf Deutsch?

☐ hinteres Haus ☐ wieder zu Hause

b) Look at the picture. What can you see?
Sieh dir das Bild an. Was kannst du sehen?

I can see ...

c) Listen and read along. 2
Höre zu und lies mit.

Jasmine: Hello Sandeep. How are you?

Sandeep: Oh, hi Jasmine. I'm fine. How was your holiday?

Jasmine: Fantastic! We went to Paris.

Sandeep: Cool!

Jasmine: And look at this photo. Me and Jason were on the beach in France.

Sandeep: Oh, it looks really windy there.

Jasmine: Yeah, it was windy and cloudy. We went swimming and played beach volleyball. And what about you?

Sandeep: It was often cold and rainy here. So I helped my parents in the shop.

Jasmine: And what about Megan and Ben?

Sandeep: I met Ben yesterday. We went to the cinema.

Jasmine: Great! Let's phone Megan and Ben.

d) Read again. Then put the pictures in the correct order.
Lies den Dialog erneut. Dann bringe die Bilder in die richtige Reihenfolge.

e) Now match the pictures and the sentences.
Ordne nun die Bilder den Sätzen zu.

- Jasmine was in Paris.
- Jasmine and Jason went to the beach in France.
- Jasmine and Jason went swimming and played beach volleyball.
- Sandeep helped his parents in the shop.
- Sandeep and Ben went to the cinema.

4 Weather words

a) Match the words and the pictures. Draw lines.
Ordne die Wörter den Bildern zu. Verbinde.

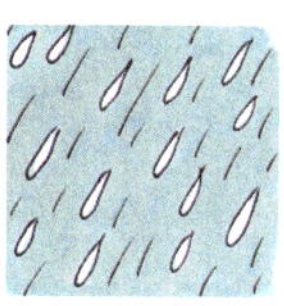

windy

cold

sunny

rainy

warm

cloudy

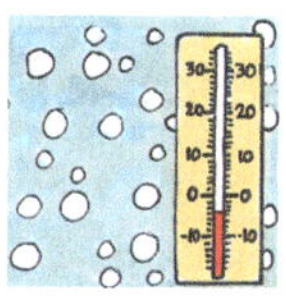

b) Listen and repeat. 3
Höre zu und sprich nach.

6 Ben's holidays

What did Ben do in his holidays? Unscramble the sentences.
Was hat Ben in seinen Ferien gemacht? Ordne die Sätze.

1.

Ben – in Wales. – was

Ben was in Wales.

2.

stayed – He – at a campsite.

3.

a castle. – He – visited

4.

watched – He – dolphins.

5.

He – minigolf. – played

LAND & LEUTE

Die britischen Inseln

Wusstest du, dass das Vereinigte Königreich Großbritannien und Nordirland (*United Kingdom of Great Britain and Northern Ireland, UK*) aus England, Schottland (*Scotland*), Wales und Nordirland (*Northern Ireland*) besteht?

Kennst du die Hauptstadt von England?
Schau dir die Karte vorne im Buch an. Wie heißen die Hauptstädte von Schottland, Wales und Nordirland?

8 A postcard

a) Find your way through the maze. You can only step on verbs.
Finde deinen Weg durch das Labyrinth. Du kannst nur auf Verben vorankommen.

Start ↓	England	sister	job	shop
visited	holiday	weather	cinema	brother
castle	went	hotel	day	dog
campsite	walked	pool	night	cat
city	parents	were	were	had
beach	restaurant	party	London	**End**

b) Read the postcard. What is it about?
Lies die Postkarte. Worum geht es?

☐ birthdays ☐ holidays ☐ sports

12th August

Dear Sandeep,

Wales is a cool place.

Yesterday we v________________ a famous castle.

Today we w________________ to the top of Mount Snowdon. We w________________ for four hours.

We w________________ very lucky.

There w________________ no clouds in the sky and we h________________ a great view from the top.

Bye for now,

Ben

Sandeep Chopra
87 Camden High Street
London
NW1 0JH

c) Complete the postcard with the verbs from a)
Vervollständige die Postkarte mit den Verben von a).

d) Erzähle deinem Partner/deiner Partnerin auf Deutsch von Bens Ferien.

9 I didn't

a) Listen to the rap. What did the boy do in the holidays? Tick the correct picture. 4

Höre dir den Rap an. Was hat der Junge in den Ferien gemacht? Mache ein Häkchen an das richtige Bild.

I didn't watch films at the cinema each day,
I didn't go out to the playground to play.

I didn't go swimming or eat ice cream a lot,
I didn't read books in a sunny spot.

I didn't play football or tennis outside,
I didn't have a picnic or go on a bike ride.

I didn't go abroad or to anywhere hot,
now that I think about it I didn't do a lot.

I didn't join a band or become a top drummer,
but man,
I played lots of computer games this summer!

b) Underline what the boy did in his holidays (green). Underline what he didn't do (red).

Unterstreiche, was der Junge in seinen Ferien gemacht hat (grün). Unterstreiche, was er nicht gemacht hat (rot).

c) Listen to the rap again and act it out.

Höre dir den Rap erneut an und spiele ihn nach.

d) **Work with a partner. Ask and answer questions.**
Arbeitet zu zweit. Stellt Fragen und beantwortet sie.

Did you watch films this summer?

Yes, I did.

No, I didn't.

11 Lynn's holiday diary

a) **Read about Lynn's Sunday in Germany.**
Lies über Lynns Sonntag in Deutschland.

Du kannst dir den Text auch anhören. 5

Sunday, 16th August

In the morning it was sunny.
We hired bikes and went for a ride along the River Main.
My cousin came with us. He is thirteen and so nice!
We saw Frankfurt's fantastic skyscrapers.
After the ride we were really hungry. So we went to a restaurant.
In the afternoon we went to the zoo. I loved the beautiful tigers.
Now I'm really tired. I was very happy today.
It was a wonderful day!

b) **Read again and complete the sentences.**
Lies noch einmal und vervollständige die Sätze.

1. In the morning it was s ___ ___ ___ ___.
2. Lynn and her parents hired b ___ ___ ___ ___ and went for a r ___ ___ ___.
3. Her c ___ ___ ___ ___ ___ came with them. He is thirteen and very n ___ ___ ___.
4. They saw Frankfurt's fantastic s ___ ___ ___ ___ ___ ___ ___ ___ ___ ___.
5. After the ride they w ___ ___ ___ to a restaurant.
6. In the afternoon they went to the z ___ ___.

12 Word groups

Read the words and find 6 that belong to the word field. Circle.
Lies die Wörter und finde 6, die zu einem Wortfeld gehören. Kreise sie ein.

1. weather

sunny	snowy	warm	cold
happy	windy	T-shirt	money
colour	beach	blue	rainy

2. places

red	restaurant	zoo	car
castle	go	museum	cold
bike	beach	dog	cinema

3. activities

book	animal	place	food
teacher	family	visit	walk
play	go	meet	watch

14 Choose an activity

- **Find words for the letters.**
  Finde Wörter für die Buchstaben.

  Schau in der Wörterliste ab S. 114 nach.

B ______________________
E ______________________
A ______________________
C ______________________
H ______________________

- **Make a word snake with holiday words. Then let your partner find the words.**
  Erstelle eine Wortschlange mit Wörtern zum Thema Ferien. Lass deinen Partner/deine Partnerin die Wörter finden.

16 Target task: Your holidays

a) Choose and circle one or more ideas in the boxes.
Wähle eine oder mehrere Ideen aus den Kästchen aus und kreise sie ein.

I was ... at home | on a farm | in the park | at the beach | at the zoo | ... in England | in Spain | in Turkey | ...	**The weather was ...** nice | warm | sunny | bad | cold | rainy | windy | ...
I ... played football | went swimming | visited a friend | watched TV | went shopping | met my friends | played with my sister/brother | played video games | had lots of ice cream | ...	**My holidays were ...** great | super | OK | exciting | cool | too short | boring | ...

b) Complete the text. Vervollständige den Text.

My summer holidays

I was .

The weather was .

I

.

My holidays were .

c) Present your text to the class. Präsentiere deinen Text in der Klasse.

1 Back to school

Du kannst dir die Wörter auch anhören. 6

a) **Read the words in the yellow box. Sort them into the blue boxes.**
Lies die Wörter im gelben Kasten. Sortiere sie in die blauen Kästen.

pencil | French | PE | music | bin | scissors | folder | teacher | art | student | book | classmate | ruler | science | whiteboard | desk | map | ICT | chair | rubber | history | pencil case | pen | English | maths

schoolbag:

people:

subjects:

classroom:

b) **Can you add more words?** Kannst du noch mehr Wörter ergänzen?

LAND & LEUTE

Schulsystem in Großbritannien
Für britische Kinder beginnt die Grundschule (*primary school*), wenn sie vier oder fünf Jahre alt sind. Anschließend geht es auf eine weiterführende Schule (*secondary school*). Die meisten Schülerinnen und Schüler besuchen dabei eine staatliche Schule, zum Beispiel eine Gesamtschule. Auch Haverstock ist eine Gesamtschule.

Was weißt du über das Schulsystem in Deutschland oder in anderen Ländern?

3 Haverstock School

a) Look at the website. What is it about?
Schau dir die Webseite an. Worum geht es?

☐ a school ☐ a sports club ☐ a city

b) Read the website. Lies die Webseite.

Welcome to Haverstock

Haverstock School in London has got more than 1,000 students.

Library
At Haverstock School you can find lots of books.
The library is open from 7:30 a.m. to 4:30 p.m.

Sports
In the gym students can take part in basketball, indoor cricket, badminton, indoor football and other activities.

Clubs
There are lots of clubs and activities: ICT clubs, games clubs (chess, darts, snooker) and many sports clubs.

Uniforms
Students have to wear school uniforms: a grey shirt, a dark blue blazer and a tie, black trousers or a black skirt and black shoes.

c) Read the website again. Underline the correct answer.
Lies die Webseite erneut und unterstreiche die richtige Antwort.

1. There are more than 1,000 / 2,000 students at Haverstock School.
2. At Haverstock school there is a library / swimming pool.
3. In the gym you can take part in chess / indoor football.
4. At Haverstock School they have got lots of clubs / cafeterias.
5. Students wear jeans and a sweatshirt / school uniforms.

5 What's different, what's the same?

a) Read the information about Haverstock School.
Lies die Informationen über die Haverstock Schule.

Haverstock School	
number of students	more than 1,000
uniform	shirt, blazer, tie, trousers, black shoes, skirt
clubs	ICT clubs, games clubs, sports clubs
sports	basketball, indoor cricket, indoor football, badminton

b) Look up all the words you don't know.
Schlage alle Wörter nach, die du nicht kennst.

Schau in der Wörterliste ab S. 114 nach.

c) Complete the table about your school.
Vervollständige die Tabelle über deine Schule.

Our school	
number of students	
uniform	
clubs	
sports	

d) Talk to a partner about what is different and what is the same.
Sprecht zu zweit darüber, was anders und was gleich ist.

An der Haverstock Schule sind mehr als 1000 Schülerinnen und Schüler.

An unserer Schule sind ... Schülerinnen und Schüler.

6 School sounds

Listen to the dialogues. Where do they take place? Number.
Höre dir die Dialoge an. Wo finden sie statt? Nummeriere sie.

9 Haverstock School Library

Sieh dir die Informationen zur Schulbücherei an.
Beantworte die Fragen von jemandem, der kein Englisch versteht.

Haverstock School Library

Opening times:

Mon – Fri 7:30 a.m. – 4:30 p.m.

Students can use the library for reading and borrowing books and using the computers.

There are 30 computers and 30 laptops with filtered Internet access.

They may not be used for games and chat rooms.

Students may borrow up to three books at a time.

Wann hat die Schulbücherei geöffnet?

Was kann man in der Schulbücherei machen?

Wie viele Computer und Laptops gibt es?

Wie viele Bücher darf man ausleihen?

10 A new classmate

a) Listen. Match the questions and the answers. 8
Höre zu. Ordne die Fragen und Antworten zu.

What's your name?

How old are you?

Where are you from?

Have you got any brothers or sisters?

What are your hobbies?

Have you got a pet?

What sports do you like?

Music and playing video games.

No, I haven't.

I'm from Cardiff.

Hello, I'm Josh.

Judo, basketball and football.

I'm twelve years old.

Yes, two guinea pigs – Mickey and Mouse.

b) Listen again and check.
Höre zu und überprüfe.

c) Read the dialogue with a partner. Lest den Dialog zu zweit.

13 Target task: Your school

a) **Collect words about your school.** Sammle Wörter über deine Schule.

number of students	school clubs	favourite subjects	other things (rooms, places, activities, ...)

b) **Make a poster about your school.** Mache ein Poster über deine Schule.

My school

The name of my school is ______________________________.

There are ______________________ students at my school.

The school clubs are ______________________________

______________________________.

My favourite subjects are ______________________________

______________________________.

Other things: There is ______________________________

______________________________.

c) **Present your poster in class.** Präsentiere dein Poster in der Klasse.

Theme 2

Around London

In diesem *Theme* beschäftigst du dich mit ...

- den Sehenswürdigkeiten in London,
- Wegbeschreibungen,
- dem Londoner Zoo,
- Tieren.

2

1

1 London

What comes to your mind when you think of London?
Was fällt dir ein, wenn du an London denkst?

I think of ...

2 Famous sights

Listen and read along. Then match the sentences with the pictures. 9
Höre zu und lies mit. Dann ordne die Sätze den Bildern zu.

☐ The Queen lives at Buckingham Palace when she is in London.

☐ There are a lot of shops, stalls, acrobats and musicians in Covent Garden.

☐ The London Eye is a very big wheel. From the top you have an amazing view over London.

☐ Big Ben is a tower with a clock inside.

☐ Tower Bridge is a famous bridge over the River Thames.

☐ Hyde Park is the perfect place to sit in the sun and have a picnic.

4 What can you do there?

a) Complete the sentences with verbs from the box.
Vervollständige die Sätze mit den Verben aus dem Kasten.

visit | watch | see | enjoy | listen to

1. You can v ___ ___ ___ ___ Buckingham Palace.
2. You can l ___ ___ ___ ___ ___ ___ ___ the sound of Big Ben.
3. You can e ___ ___ ___ ___ a great view from the London Eye.
4. You can w ___ ___ ___ ___ Tower Bridge open up.
5. You can s ___ ___ stalls, acrobats and musicians at Covent Garden.

b) Dein Freund/Deine Freundin spricht kein Englisch. Erzähle ihm/ihr auf Deutsch, was man unternehmen kann.

5 Where to go in London

a) Match the words and the pictures. Draw lines.
Ordne die Wörter und die Bilder zu. Verbinde.

watch

enjoy

visit

listen to

go on

see

b) Talk to a partner. Arbeitet zu zweit.

Where can you go when it is sunny?

... it is rainy?
... you have no money?
... you want to see the Queen?
... you want to have a great view?
... you want to see stalls and musicians?
... you like bridges?
...

You can go to Hyde Park.

... visit Tower Bridge.
... go on a bus tour.
... listen to Big Ben.
... enjoy a great view from the London Eye.
... watch Tower Bridge open up.
...

9 Your favourite sights

a) Look at the photos and match them with the sentences.
Schau dir die Fotos an und ordne sie den Sätzen zu.

Du kannst dir die Texte auch anhören. 10

1 
2 
3 
4 
5 

☐ You want to meet the Queen or Ryan Gosling? Then come to Madame Tussauds!

☐ Come and see the fantastic world of Harry Potter. See all the costumes from the films. Visit the Harry Potter Museum!

☐ Are you a football fan? Visit Wembley Stadium and take a tour!

☐ Do you like animals? Visit London Zoo and enjoy a nice day!

☐ Do you like fantastic buildings? Then visit the Tower of London!

b) Which three sights would you like to see? Talk to a partner.
Welche drei Sehenswürdigkeiten möchtest du gerne sehen? Arbeitet zu zweit.

What's your number one sight?

My number one is the London Eye. What about you?

I want to visit Big Ben.

Good idea. I'd like to visit Tower Bridge.

LAND & LEUTE

Unterwegs in London

London ist eine sehr große Stadt. Sie ist mehr als zweimal so groß wie Berlin. Zum Glück gibt es dort ein weit verzweigtes U-Bahnnetz – die *London Underground*.
Die Londoner nennen ihre U-Bahn *the Tube* (Röhre).
Damit kommt man überall gut und schnell hin.
Willst du mehr von London sehen, solltest du unbedingt die roten *double-deckers* (Doppeldeckerbusse) nehmen und vom Oberdeck eine *sightseeing tour* (Stadtrundfahrt) genießen.
Weltberühmt sind auch die meist schwarzen *cabs* (Taxis).

Achtung beim Überqueren der Straße – in Großbritannien herrscht Linksverkehr.

Welche Verkehrsmittel gibt es bei dir?

10 On the London Underground

Sieh dir die Informationen in einer Londoner U-Bahn-Station an. Beantworte die Fragen von jemandem, der kein Englisch versteht.

1

2

3

1. Was soll man auf der Rolltreppe beachten?
2. Was ist verboten?
3. Wohin geht es, wenn man dem Schild folgt?

11 A chat

a) Read the chat between Ben and Jasmine. What are their plans?
Lies den Chat zwischen Ben und Jasmine. Was sind ihre Pläne?

☐ a sightseeing tour ☐ a party

b) What does 'bff' mean?
Was bedeutet ‚bff'?

☐ best friends forever

☐ beautiful friendly friend

c) Do you know any more text messaging short forms?
Kennst du noch mehr Chat-Abkürzungen?

____

12 A sightseeing tour

a) Listen to the tour guide. Underline the sights he is talking about. 11
Höre dem Reiseführer zu. Unterstreiche die Sehenswürdigkeiten, die er nennt.

Buckingham Palace | Big Ben | Hyde Park | Covent Garden | London Zoo | the River Thames | the Palace of Westminster | Tower Bridge | the London Eye | the Tower of London

b) Listen again and underline the correct answer.
Höre erneut zu und unterstreiche die richtige Antwort.

1. The weather is	**rainy**	**sunny** .
2. Some people call Buckingham Palace	**Buck House**	**Ham Palace** .
3. Hyde Park is a good place to	**relax**	**play golf** .
4. Ben, Lynn and Jasmine get off at	**the Tower of London**	**London Zoo** .

14 Choose an activity

- **Do the crossword about London sights.**
  Mache das Kreuzworträtsel über die Londoner Sehenswürdigkeiten.

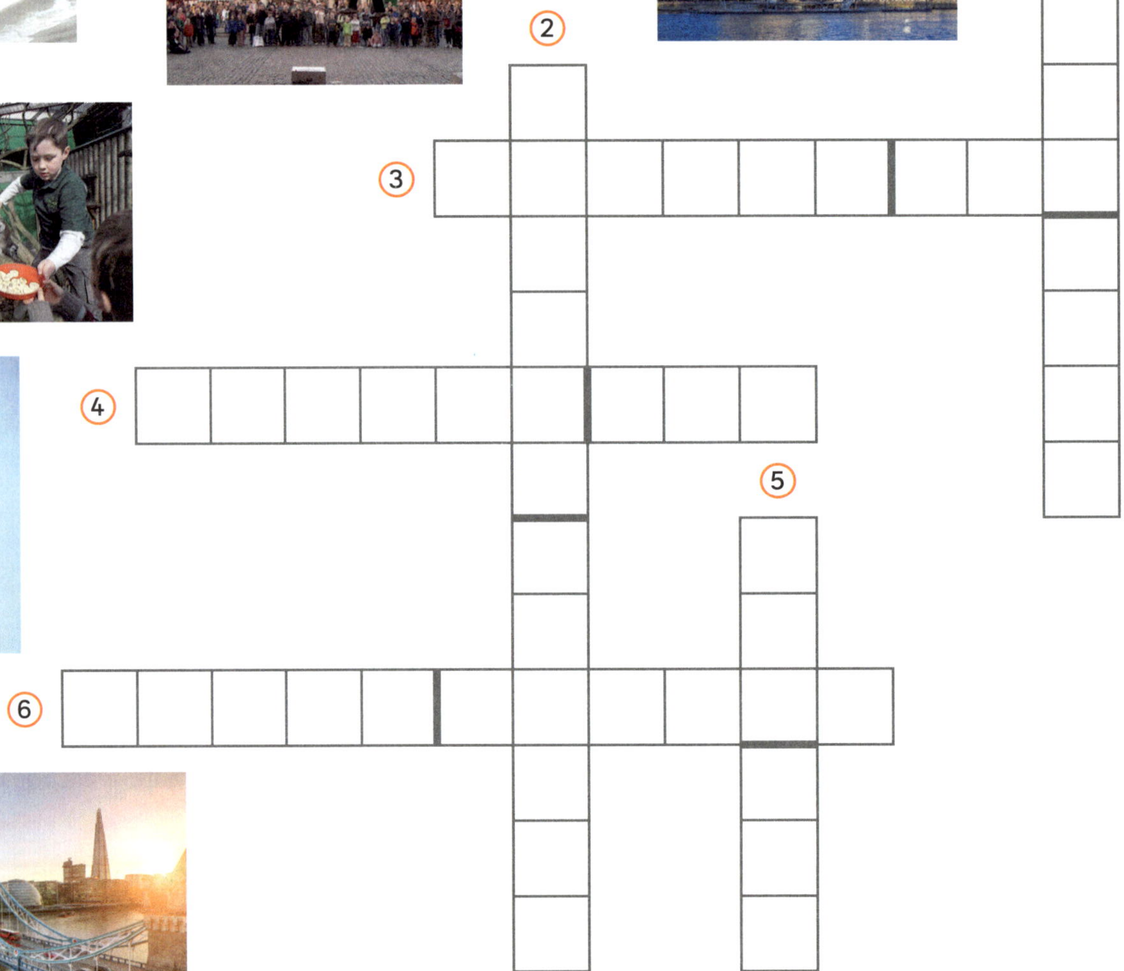

- **Complete the sudoku.** Vervollständige das Sudoku.

Big Ben	Hyde Park	Tower Bridge	
	London Zoo		Big Ben
Hyde Park			Tower Bridge
	Tower Bridge	Big Ben	

15 Target task: An audio guide for London

a) **Work with a partner. Choose a London sight.**
Arbeitet zu zweit. Wählt eine Londoner Sehenswürdigkeit.

____

b) **Then collect information on it. Look for information on pages 22-24.**
Dann sammelt Informationen dazu. Sucht nach Informationen auf den Seiten 22-24.

____

____

____

c) **Complete the text with your information.**
Ergänzt den Text mit euren Informationen.

Hello and welcome to London!

Our names are ______________ and ______________

and we are your tour guides.

Today we are at ______________________.

Did you know that ______________________

______________________________?

Enjoy your visit!

d) **Ask your teacher to check your text.**
Lasst euren Text von eurem Lehrer/
eurer Lehrerin korrigieren.

e) **Practise reading your text.**
Übt das Lesen eures Textes.

f) **Record your text.**
Nehmt euren Text auf.

1 Two pictures

In picture A
I can see ...

a) **Look at the pictures. What can you see?**
Sieh dir die Bilder an. Beschreibe, was du siehst.

A

B

b) **What are the people doing? Tick.**
Was machen die Leute? Mache ein Häkchen.

Du kannst dir die richtigen Lösungen anhören. 12

Picture A

- [ ] Jasmine is looking at her phone.
- [ ] The children are buying tickets.
- [ ] A car is parking on the right.
- [ ] A man is selling balloons.

Picture B

- [ ] Lynn is talking to a man.
- [ ] The young man next to Lynn is eating an ice cream.
- [ ] A man is talking on the phone.
- [ ] A woman is buying a T-shirt.

2 What happened?

a) Listen and read along. 13
Höre zu und lies mit.

Ben: Where is Lynn? It's 3:15 already.
Jasmine: I don't know. She wanted to buy some souvenirs at Camden Market and then come right here.
Ben: But does she know how to get here?
Jasmine: No, she doesn't. But she wanted to follow the directions on her phone.
Ben: So why don't you phone her?
Jasmine: OK, OK. … I can't reach Lynn on her phone.
Ben: Maybe she forgot it at your house.
Jasmine: No, she didn't. She texted me from the market an hour ago.
Ben: Then text her and tell her to hurry up … please.

Lynn: Damn! My phone is dead. How do I get to London Zoo now? … Excuse me, can you tell me the way to London Zoo, please?
Man: Let's see. Ah, OK. We're on Camden High Street now. So …

b) Read again. Then find the correct ending. Draw lines.
Lies den Text erneut. Dann finde das richtige Ende. Verbinde.

1. Lynn wanted to	is dead.
2. She wanted to follow	the way to the zoo.
3. Jasmine can't	reach Lynn on her phone.
4. Lynn's phone	the directions on her phone.
5. The man can tell Lynn	buy souvenirs at Camden Market.

c) Was ist das Problem? Erzähle es deinem Partner/deiner Partnerin auf Deutsch.

3 The way to London Zoo

a) Listen and number the sentences. 14

Höre zu und nummeriere die Sätze.

- ☐ Turn right.
- ☐ Turn left.
- ☐ Go straight on.
- ☐ It's on the left.
- ☐ It's on the right.
- ☐ Cross the street.

b) Read the sentences and match them with the pictures.

Lies die Sätze und ordne sie den Bildern zu.

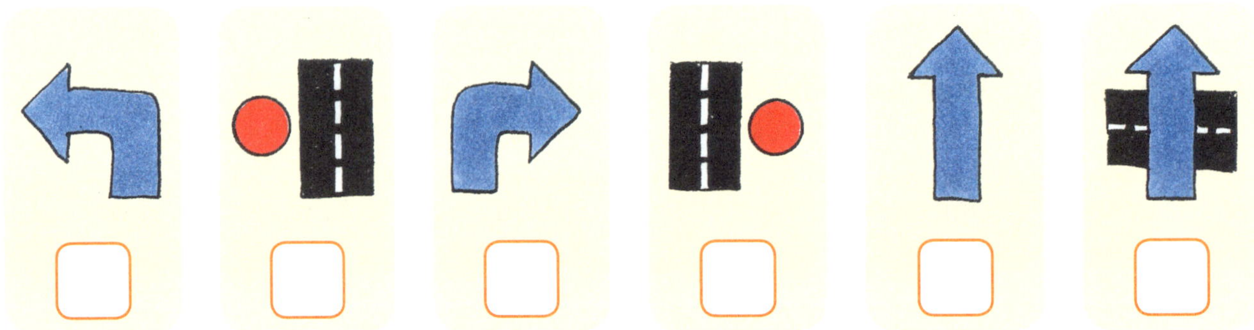

c) Listen to the man telling Lynn the way to London Zoo. Draw the route. 15

Höre dem Mann zu, der Lynn den Weg beschreibt. Zeichne den Weg ein.

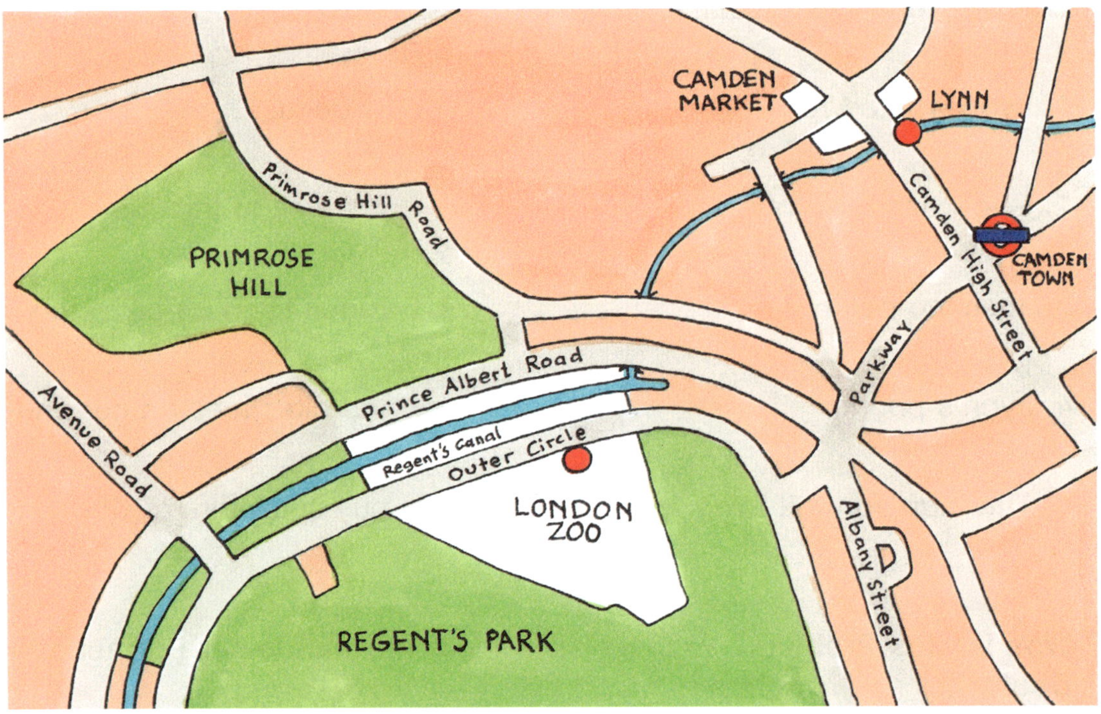

4 Giving directions

a) **Listen. Find the routes on the map.** 16
Höre zu. Finde die Wege auf der Karte.

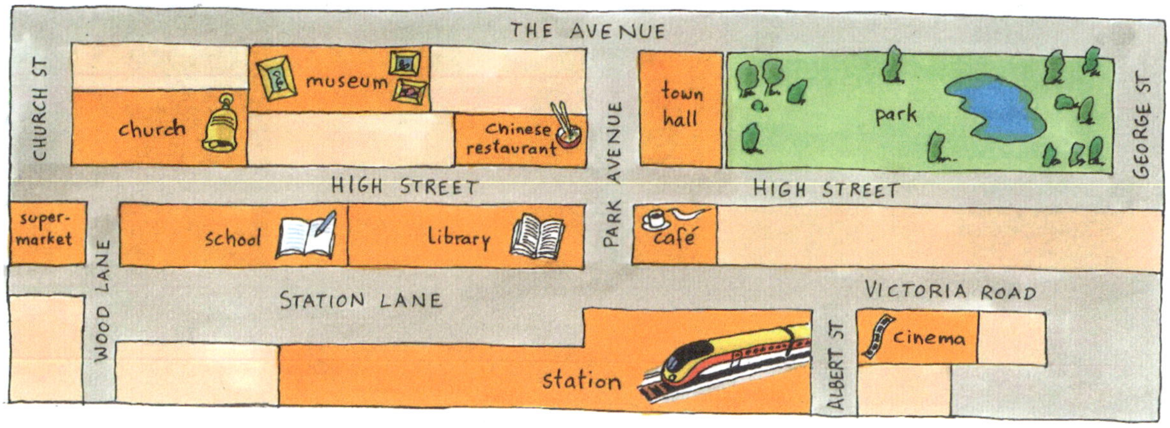

b) **Where do you get to?** Wo kommst du an?

The woman is at the ______________________________.

The man is at the ______________________________.

5 Together again

a) **Listen and number.** 17
Höre zu und nummeriere.

☐ Hi Lynn, why didn't you phone us?

☐ Sorry, my phone was dead.

☐ How did you get here?

☐ Yes, I did. It's so cool there.

☐ Did you enjoy shopping at Camden Market?

☐ I asked someone. He told me the way.

b) **Read the dialogue with a partner.**
Lest den Dialog zu zweit.

6 Animals at London Zoo

Match the photos. Ordne die Fotos einander zu.

7 Lunch for the animals

What do these animals eat? Underline in the correct colour.
Was essen diese Tiere? Unterstreiche in der richtigen Farbe.

grass

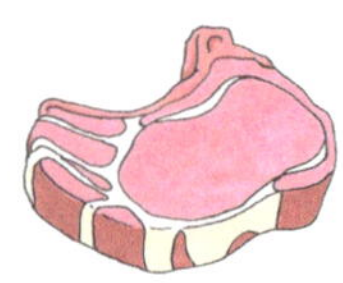
meat

plants

fruit

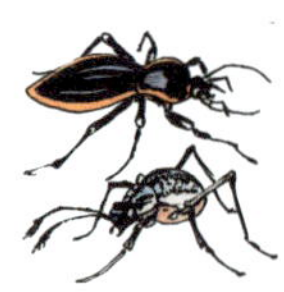
insects

leaves

fish

roots

8 Lions

a) **Listen and point.** 18
Höre zu und zeige.

b) **Match the numbers and the words.**
Ordne die Zahlen den Wörtern zu.

1 back	☐ ear	☐ head	☐ mane
☐ tail	☐ paw	☐ fur	☐ leg

c) **Find 6 things that animals can do. Circle.** Finde 6 Dinge, die Tiere tun können. Umkreise sie.

run	climb	ear
food	eat	write
fly	jump	fruit
read	phone	swim

d) **Find 7 words that describe animals. Circle.** Finde 7 Wörter, die Tiere beschreiben. Umkreise sie.

fast	big	strong
garage	car	brown
small	house	tree
tall	dangerous	flower

9 Which animal is it?

Listen and tick. 19
Höre zu und mache ein Häkchen.

1.	☐ tiger	☐ giraffe	☐ elephant
2.	☐ gorilla	☐ lion	☐ snake
3.	☐ zebra	☐ penguin	☐ hippo

11 A day out

> I can see **a gorilla**.

a) Look at the pictures. What can you see?
Sieh dir die Bilder an. Beschreibe, was du siehst.

b) Listen and point at the pictures. 20
Höre zu und zeige auf die Bilder.

- ☐ I'm Gernot the gorilla and I'm new at London Zoo. Last Monday I wanted to see some famous sights, so I went on a day out.
- ☐ I really enjoyed watching the acrobats at Covent Garden.
- ☐ First I took the Tube. There were lots of people.
- ☐ I felt hungry so I went to Hyde Park and sat under a tree. I ate some leaves. A woman gave me a banana.
- ☐ Next I went for a ride on the London Eye. It was very exciting.
- ☐ Then I went to a restaurant and had a meal. A man showed me the way back to the zoo. I had an exciting day, but I'm happy to be back home.
- ☐ Then I went to Buckingham Palace. Someone took a photo of me and one of the guards.

c) Read the texts. Match the pictures and the texts.
Lies die Texte. Ordne die Texte den Bildern zu.

12 Target task: Your animal book

a) Choose an animal and make a fact file.
Suche dir ein Tier aus und schreibe einen Steckbrief.

Name: ____________________

What they look like: ____________________

____

____

What they eat: ____________________

This is interesting about them:

____

____

Name: tiger

What they look like: fur is orange with black stripes, long tail

What they eat: meat

This is interesting about them:

can swim, like water

b) Use the fact file to write a text for an animal book. Look at the example for help.
Verwende den Steckbrief, um einen Text für ein Tierbuch zu schreiben. Sieh dir das Beispiel an, wenn du Hilfe brauchst.

Schreibe deinen Text auf ein Blatt Papier.

Tigers

Tigers come from Asia.
They eat meat.
They can swim and like water.
They have orange fur with black stripes.

c) Put your pages together to make an animal book.
Fügt eure Seiten zusammen, um ein Tierbuch zu erstellen.

Theme 3

Dreams

In diesem *Theme* beschäftigst du dich mit ...

- der Zukunft und Zukunftsträumen,
- Berufen und Berufswünschen,
- Vorbildern und Helden.

1 Kitchen talk

a) Look at the picture. What can you see?
Sieh dir das Bild an. Was kannst du sehen?

I can see ...

There is ...

b) Listen and read along. What are they talking about? 21

Höre zu und lies mit. Worüber sprechen sie?

☐ mobile phones ☐ horoscopes

c) Match the English with the German sentences. Number.
Ordne die englischen den deutschen Sätzen zu. Nummeriere sie.

- [ ] Aber da stehen wirklich nette Sachen drin.
- [ ] Es ist lustig, glaub mir.
- [ ] Vergiß es!
- [ ] Hör auf, Ben! Ich glaube nicht an Horoskope. Das ist Quatsch.
- [ ] Hör zu, Sarah! Hier ist dein Horoskop für den nächsten Monat.

3 Talking on the phone

a) Look at the pictures. Say what you see.
Sieh dir die Bilder an. Sag, was du siehst.

b) Listen to the dialogue and read along. 22
Höre dir den Dialog an und lies mit.

Ben: Hi Megan.

Megan: Hi Ben. What are you doing?

Ben: I'm looking at the horoscopes.

Megan: Ah, OK. What does your horoscope say?

Ben: It says: Don't worry about the future.

Megan: So, what will you do in the future?

Ben: I'm sure I'll get a good job.
I think I'll work with computers.

Megan: Sounds good. I love animals so I'll be a vet.

Ben: Cool!

Megan: Will you marry someone?

Ben: Maybe I'll marry a nice woman.
But I won't have four kids. What about you?

Megan: I won't marry anyone. But I'll always have a dog and great friends like you.

Ben: Aww, that's nice!

b) Underline Megan's and Ben's future plans. (Megan green, Ben blue)
Unterstreiche Megans und Bens Zukunftspläne. (Megan grün, Ben blau)

c) What will they do? (✓) What won't they do? (✗)
Was werden sie tun? (✓) Was werden sie nicht tun? (✗)

4 Ideas about the future

Match the sentences. Then talk to a partner about Megan's and Ben's future.
Verbinde die Sätze. Dann sprecht zu zweit über Megans und Bens Zukunft.

Megan will	marry anyone.
She won't	be a vet.
She will always	have a dog and great friends.

Ben will	have four kids.
He will	work with computers.
He won't	marry a nice woman.

5 When I'm 25

a) **Write sentences about Jasmine's future.** Schreibe Sätze über Jasmines Zukunft.

marry a nice man and have two children | play professional basketball | have a fast car

I will ______________________________.

I will ______________________________.

I won't ______________________________.

b) **Now write about your ideas.** Nun schreibe über deine Ideen.

I will ______________________________.

I will ______________________________.

I won't ______________________________.

8 A horoscope

a) **Complete the first sentence. Cover it and give your book to your partner. Go on like this.**
Vervollständige den ersten Satz. Leg etwas über ihn und gib dein Heft deinem Partner/deiner Partnerin. Mach so weiter.

1. Next Wednesday you will go ______________________.
2. You will meet ______________________.
3. You will feel happy because you will ______________________.
4. On Sunday you will see ______________________.
5. The weather will be ______________________.
6. You will have ______________________.
7. You will ______________________.
8. You will always/never ______________________.

1. shopping | cycling | to a football match | to a concert | on a blind date | ...
2./4. Taylor Swift | Dwayne Johnson | your maths teacher | ...
3. win the lottery | meet a boy/girl | fall in love with ... | meet a famous ... | ...
5. sunny | rainy | cloudy | snowy | cold | bad | ...
6. a lot of money | three children | a big car | problems with ... | ...
7. have a picnic | go on a shopping tour | do sports | ...
8. be happy | be rich | be famous | ...

b) **Read the horoscope to your partner.**
Lies das Horoskop deinem Partner/deiner Partnerin vor.

10 Jobs

a) Listen and repeat. 23
Höre zu und sprich nach.

1. bus driver

2. bricklayer

3. shop assistant

4. hairdresser

5. police officer

6. video game designer

7. mechanic

8. nurse

b) Which job is it? Look at a) and number.
Welcher Beruf ist es? Schau dir a) an und nummeriere.

☐ Mechaniker/in	☐ Polizist/in
☐ Friseur/in	☐ Maurer/in
☐ Busfahrer/in	☐ Verkäufer/in
☐ Videospielentwickler/in	☐ Krankenschwester/Krankenpfleger

c) What job would you like to have? Talk to a partner.
Welchen Beruf hättest du gerne? Sprecht zu zweit.

What will you be?

I'll be a nurse.

11 What are their jobs?

a) **Find 7 jobs in the wordsearch.** Finde 7 Berufe im Rätsel.

M	E	C	H	A	N	I	C	Q	Y	D	R	T	D
A	V	D	W	C	G	Y	L	O	O	G	T	S	S
W	Q	A	B	U	S	D	R	I	V	E	R	E	N
Z	F	S	T	T	D	C	P	N	U	R	S	E	B
S	H	O	P	A	S	S	I	S	T	A	N	T	J
F	R	H	A	I	R	D	R	E	S	S	E	R	I
I	C	F	C	S	S	E	A	H	O	X	E	T	U
G	P	O	L	I	C	E	O	F	F	I	C	E	R
B	R	I	C	K	L	A	Y	E	R	J	W	L	P

b) **Complete the sentences. Use the words in the box.**
Vervollständige die Sätze. Benutze die Wörter im Kasten.

helps people in trouble | builds houses | takes care of ill people | cuts your hair | repairs cars | drives buses | sells things | designs computer games

1. A mechanic ______________________________.
2. A bus driver ______________________________.
3. A bricklayer ______________________________.
4. A shop assistant ______________________________.
5. A police officer ______________________________.
6. A video game designer ______________________________.
7. A hairdresser ______________________________.
8. A nurse ______________________________.

15 What will happen?

a) **Answer the questions. Take notes.** Beantworte die Fragen. Mache Notizen.

Where will you live when you are 25?	
What car will you have?	
Who will you marry?	
How many children will you have?	

b) **Ask and answer the questions from a) with a partner.**
Fragt und beantwortet die Fragen von a) zu zweit.

Where will you live when you are 25?

I'll live in Berlin.

16 Target task: Your future

a) **Make a poster about your future in 20 years. Collect ideas first.**
Erstelle ein Poster über deine Zukunft in 20 Jahren. Sammle erst Ideen.

Übertrage deine Ideen auf ein Blatt Papier und ergänze Bilder.

What I will be:
I will be a mechanic, nurse, ...

What I will have:
I will have a dog, five children, ...

What I will do:
I will play hockey, watch a lot of films, ...

Where I will live:
I will live in a house, in London, ...

b) **Present your poster in class.** Präsentiere dein Poster vor der Klasse.

1 All kinds of heroes

a) Read the blog entries. Lies die Blogeinträge.

Du kannst dir die Blogeinträge auch anhören. 24

Megan

My hero is my dog. Sir Barks-A-Lot is always friendly. He listens to my problems. He makes me feel much better.

Sandeep

I'm a big football fan. My favourite player is Dele Alli. He can run really fast and he scores fantastic goals.

Ben

I think my hero is my sister Sarah. She sits in a wheelchair and can't walk. She is really good at playing wheelchair basketball.

Jasmine

My hero is Tarzan. He lived in Africa and protected the jungle and the animals in it.

b) Who are their heroes? Circle. Wer sind ihre Helden? Umkreise.

c) Talk to a partner. Sprecht zu zweit.

Sandeep's hero is a football player.

2 Your hero or favourite person

a) **Who is your hero or favourite person? Complete the speech bubbles.**
Wer ist dein Held oder Lieblingsmensch? Ergänze die Sprechblasen.

Du kannst deinen Lehrer/deine Lehrerin nach weiteren Vokabeln fragen.

My hero / favourite person is

_______________________________.

Trage den Namen deines Helden oder Lieblingsmenschen ein.

He/She lives in

_______________________________.

my house | Hamburg | Germany | the USA | England | ...

He/She is

_______________________________.

cool | interesting | friendly | nice | funny | clever | good-looking | ...

He/She can

_______________________________.

play the guitar | play football | sing well | act well | run fast | ...

I like him/her because he/she

_______________________________.

listens to my problems | sings nice songs | plays football very well | scores a lot of goals | protects nature | has lots of good ideas | ...

b) **Then tell your partner.** Dann sprecht zu zweit.

4 Grace Darling

a) Look at the pictures. Say what you see.
Schau dir dir Bilder an. Sag, was du siehst.

Du kannst dir die Geschichte auch anhören. 25

b) Read the story about Grace. Lies die Geschichte über Grace.

Grace Darling, her parents and her brothers and sisters lived in a lighthouse.
Mr Darling was the lighthouse keeper.

In 1838 there was a terrible storm.

Grace and her father brought the survivors safely to the lighthouse. Mrs Darling and her daughters cooked soup and made tea for everyone.

c) **Find the English words in the text.** Finde die englischen Wörter im Text.

Leuchtturmwärter: ____________________

Sturm: ____________________

Schiffswrack: ____________________

Überlebende/r: ____________________

rudern: ____________________

vorsichtig: ____________________

d) **Read the story again. Then answer the questions.**
Lies die Geschichte erneut. Dann beantworte die Fragen.

to the lighthouse | a shipwreck | in 1838 | by boat | Grace Darling and her family | Grace and her father

1. Who lived in the lighthouse? ____________________
2. When was the terrible storm? ____________________
3. What did Grace see from her window? ____________________
4. Who wanted to help the people? ____________________
5. How did Grace get to the shipwreck? ____________________
6. Where did Grace and her father bring the people? ____________________

5 What are the words?

a) Complete the words. You can find help in the box.
Vervollständige die Wörter. Du findest Hilfe im Kasten.

keeper | row | careful | save | shipwreck | lighthouse | storm | survivor

1. r _o_ _w_
2. s __ __ e
3. s __ __ __ m
4. s h __ p __ __ e c k
5. k __ __ p e r
6. s __ r v __ __ __ r
7. l i __ __ t h __ __ s e
8. c a __ __ f u l

b) Listen and repeat. 26
Höre zu und wiederhole.

6 Grace's story

Read the sentences and underline the correct words.
Lies die Sätze und unterstreiche die richtigen Wörter.

This is what Grace told her brothers later:

1. I could see a shipwreck from my **boat** **window**.
2. I could also see some **survivors** **whales**.
3. Father and I went out to sea in a **boat** **car**.
4. We rowed quickly to the **police** **shipwreck**.
5. The **survivors** **animals** got in the boat carefully.
6. We brought the people to the **lighthouse** **police**.
7. Mother and our sisters made **soup** **sandwiches** for everyone.
8. I'm very happy that we **saw** **helped** so many people.

8 A dramatic reading

a) Listen to Grace and her parents. How do they talk? 27
Höre Grace und ihren Eltern zu. Wie sprechen sie?

a. happily | b. loudly | c. sadly | d. quickly | e. worriedly

1. Grace talks ______.
2. Mrs Darling talks ______.
3. Grace talks ______.
4. Mr Darling talks ______.
5. Grace talks ______.

Schreibe während des Hörens die Buchstaben auf und nach dem Hören das Wort.

b) Read the speech bubbles and match them with the people.
Lies die Sprechblasen und ordne sie den Personen zu.

1. Grace
2. the survivors
3. Mrs Darling

We need to help the survivors.

Please row quickly.

Help me, please!

You saved my life.

Be careful and come back safely!

c) Work with a partner. Read the sentences in two different ways.
Arbeitet zu zweit. Lest die Sätze auf zwei verschiedene Arten.

11 How are they doing things?

Überlegt zu zweit, warum das so ist.

a) **Read the sentences. Tick the sentence that describes the picture better.**
Lies die Sätze. Mache ein Häkchen an den Satz, der das Bild besser beschreibt.

☐ They are singing.

☐ They are singing loudly.

b) **Look at the pictures.** Sieh dir die Bilder an.

c) **Complete the sentences with words from the box.**
Vervollständige die Sätze mit den Wörtern aus dem Kasten.

1. The man is driving ______________________.
2. The girl is running ______________________.
3. The woman is singing ______________________.
4. The boy is working ______________________.
5. The dog is barking ______________________.
6. The old man is walking ______________________.

carefully
dangerously
fast
hard
loudly
beautifully

13 Choose an activity

- **Find 6 words in the snake.** Finde 6 Wörter in der Schlange.

- **Do the quiz about Grace.** Löse das Rätsel über Grace.

1. Grace lived in a _ i _ _ _ _ _ _ _ e.
2. In 1838 there was a terrible s _ _ _ _.
3. Grace and her _ _ t _ e _ wanted to help the survivors.
4. They _ o _ _ d to them.
5. They brought the survivors s _ _ _ _ y to the lighthouse.

14 Target task: Your play

a) **Work in groups. Practise Grace's story from pages 48-49.**
Arbeitet in Gruppen. Übt die Geschichte über Grace von den Seiten 48-49.

Ihr braucht dazu:

einen Erzähler

Übe das Lesen des Textes mehrfach. Vielleicht schaffst du es, einige Textstellen auswendig vorzutragen.

Hintergrundgeräusche

Überlegt euch, welche Hintergrundgeräusche (Wind, Wellen, Ruder, ...) in der Geschichte vorkommen und wie man sie erzeugen kann.

Schauspieler/innen für Grace, Mr Darling, Mrs Darling, Graces Schwestern, die Schiffbrüchigen

Übt euren Text.

Schreibt ihn auf Karteikarten. Die sind hilfreich, wenn ihr mal nicht weiterwisst.

Übt die Betonung. (Wie fühlt sich die Person gerade?)

Merkt euch, nach wem ihr dran seid.

b) **Act out Grace's story.** Spielt die Geschichte über Grace vor.

Theme 4

Celebrations

In diesem *Theme* beschäftigst du dich mit ...

- **Festen und Feiern,**
- **Festen anderer Kulturen in Großbritannien,**
- **Plänen und Vorhaben in der Zukunft,**
- **Vergleichen von Gegenständen und Personen.**

A

B

C

D

1 Lots of festivals

a) **Look at the pictures of different festivals. Say what you see.**
Sieh dir die Bilder verschiedener Feste an. Sag, was du siehst.

In picture A
I can see ...

b) **Listen and repeat.** 28
Höre zu und wiederhole.

c) **Match the pictures with the correct festivals.**
Ordne die Bilder den richtigen Festen zu.

☐ Halloween	☐ Christmas	☐ Eid
☐ Mother's Day	☐ Hanukkah	☐ Easter
☐ New Year's Eve	☐ Chinese New Year	

E

F

G

H

d) Listen to two dialogues. Tick the correct festivals. 29

Höre dir zwei Dialoge an. Mache ein Häkchen an die richtigen Feste.

- ☐ Easter
- ☐ Christmas
- ☐ Halloween
- ☐ Chinese New Year
- ☐ Eid

Kennst du noch mehr Feste und Feiertage? Finde heraus, wie sie auf Englisch heißen.

2 Festival activities

Complete the sentences with the correct festivals.
Ergänze die Sätze mit den richtigen Festen.

Christmas | Chinese New Year | Easter | Halloween | Eid | New Year's Eve

1. For H __ __ __ __ __ __ __ __ children wear costumes and go from house to house.

2. At E __ __ __ __ __ children look for eggs and chocolate in the garden.

3. On N __ __ __ __ __ __'__ __ __ __ people often have parties and set off fireworks.

4. During E __ __ Muslims celebrate the end of Ramadan.

5. On C __ __ __ __ __ __ __ __ __ __ __ __ __ children get good-luck money.

6. For C __ __ __ __ __ __ __ __ people decorate a tree at home and open presents.

3 Favourite festivals

Talk to a partner. Sprecht zu zweit.

What's your favourite festival?

What festivals do you celebrate?

I like Christmas best.

I celebrate Halloween with my best friend.

LAND & LEUTE

Traditionelle Feste in Großbritannien

Die meisten Briten feiern Ostern (*Easter*) und Weihnachten (*Christmas*). Es gibt in Großbritannien auch einen Muttertag (*Mother's Day*) und den Valentinstag (Valentine's Day). Man schenkt sich Blumen oder Pralinen und verschickt Karten, ohne seinen Namen zu nennen.
Ein beliebtes Fest im Herbst ist Halloween. Die Kinder gehen verkleidet von Haus zu Haus. Sie fordern mit „Süßem oder Saurem" (*trick or treat*) Süßigkeiten.
In den meisten Gegenden Großbritanniens wird am 31. Dezember Silvester ähnlich wie in Deutschland gefeiert. Allerdings wird auf der Straße nur selten Feuerwerk gezündet.
In Großbritannien werden auch viele Feste anderer Kulturen gefeiert. Es gibt zum Beispiel eine große Parade zum Chinesischen Neujahr (*Chinese New Year*) in London.
Diwali ist ein wichtiges Fest der Inder. Lichter und Kerzen werden aufgestellt, damit die Götter den Weg in die Häuser finden. Es wird gesungen, getanzt und Feuerwerk gezündet.

Welche Feste feiert ihr in deiner Familie?

4 Sound check

a) Listen and repeat. 30
Höre zu und wiederhole.

b) Find the pairs.
Finde die Paare.

set off fireworks | wear a costume | celebrate | get presents | decorate | have a party | go to church

eine Party feiern: ______________________________

Geschenke bekommen: ______________________________

ein Feuerwerk zünden: ______________________________

ein Kostüm tragen: ______________________________

feiern: ______________________________

schmücken: ______________________________

zur Kirche gehen: ______________________________

5 It's Diwali time

a) Listen to the dialogue and read along. 31
Höre dir den Dialog an und lies mit.

Guess what's coming up soon?

Oh Neela, we all know. It's Diwali.

Exactly! I'm really looking forward to it. This year I'm going to wear my most beautiful sari, the red one.

And I'm going to wear my new green sari. Oh, I can't wait to decorate our house with fresh flowers.

We need lots of candles, too. I'm going to buy new ones next week and put them in the windows.

I'd like to invite my friend Josh to our house. Is that OK? I don't think he knows much about Diwali.

No problem. I hope he likes our traditional Indian food and sweets.

I'm pretty sure about that. And he'll love our fireworks. I'm going to call and ask him. Let's see if he's ready for Diwali.

b) Erzähle einem Partner/einer Partnerin auf Deutsch, worüber sich die Chopras unterhalten. Was haben Sandeep, Neela und die Eltern vor?

7 Plans for Diwali

a) **Complete the sentences.** Vervollständige die Sätze.

their best clothes | his room | Diwali cards for family and friends | their children presents and sweets | fireworks | Indian food

1. 

Neela is going to make

____.

2. 

Mr Chopra and Pradeep are going to buy

____.

3. 

Sandeep is going to decorate

____.

4. 

Mr and Mrs Chopra are going to give

____.

5. 

Mrs Chopra is going to cook

____.

6. 

Mr and Mrs Chopra are going to wear

____.

b) **Name three things you need for Diwali.**
Nenne drei Dinge, die man für das Diwali-Fest braucht.

____________________ ____________________ ____________________

11 Laura's email

a) Read Laura's email. Lies Lauras E-Mail.

Hello everyone,

My name is Laura and I'm from Australia. My favourite festival is Christmas.

It's on 25th December – summer in Australia.

At the beginning of December we start decorating the house and the garden.

On the 25th we meet our family and friends and give each other presents. We often meet them at the beach.

We usually wear T-shirts and shorts, because it's so hot in Australia.

We always have a barbecue and some cold drinks like coke or juice.

What's your favourite festival?

Bye for now,

Laura

b) Read the questions. Underline the answers in the text.
Lies die Fragen. Unterstreiche die Antworten im Text.

1. Where is Laura from?
2. What's her favourite festival?
3. When is it?
4. What do they wear?
5. What do they drink?
6. How do they celebrate?

c) Complete the text with the answers from b).
Vervollständige den Text mit den Antworten von b).

Laura is from ____________________.

Her favourite festival is ____________________.

It's on 25th ____________________.

She wears ____________________ and ____________________.

12 Target task: Your favourite festival

Benutze ein Wörterbuch.

a) What's your favourite festival? Choose or collect words.
Welches ist dein Lieblingsfest? Wähle Wörter aus oder sammle neue.

Name:	
When is it?	January, February, March, ...
What do you wear?	dress, skirt, best shirt, costume, ...
What do you eat?	cake, sausages, ...
What do you do?	sing songs, have a party, dress up, have fireworks, get presents, meet my family, ...

b) Now write your email. Nun schreibe deine E-Mail.

Hello everyone,

My name is ____________________ and I'm from ____________________.

My favourite festival is ______________________________.

It's in ______________________________.

I/We usually wear ______________________________.

We always/often eat ______________________________.

We ______________________________.

We also ______________________________.

What is your favourite festival?

Bye for now,

____

c) Send your email to a partner. Schicke deine E-Mail einem Partner/einer Partnerin.

1 A brilliant idea

Listen to the phone call. What is it about? Tick. 32
Höre dir den Telefonanruf an. Worum geht es? Mache ein Häkchen.

☐ Megan's birthday party ☐ a surprise party for Ben

2 Let's get started

a) Listen and read along. 33
Höre zu und lies mit.

Megan: So what do we need for the surprise party?

Sarah: I guess we need lots of sweets. And crisps, of course. At least five packets.

Megan: We should buy some sausages, too.

Sarah: We could also make some vegetable sticks. So we need a few carrots, a cucumber and some red or yellow peppers.

Sandeep: Ugh, that sounds too healthy.

Megan: You can also eat salad, Sandeep. My mum is going to make one.

Sandeep: Sounds good. What about water and lemonade? We need six bottles of each.

Sarah: You're right. And we should buy some decorations.

Megan: I guess we don't need to buy any. We've got loads of balloons and garlands in our party box. Let's have a look.

b) Underline what the kids need for the party.
Unterstreiche, was die Kinder für die Party brauchen.

c) Find the words for the pictures in the text.
Finde die Wörter für die Bilder im Text.

__________ __________ __________ __________ __________

3 What do they want to buy?

a) Match the pictures and the words. Draw lines.
Ordne die Bilder den Wörtern zu. Verbinde.

6 packets of crisps

__ packets of sausages

__ bottles of water

__ packets of sweets

__ box of vegetables

__ bottles of lemonade

b) How many things are there? Write down the numbers. Then listen and check. 34
Wie viele Dinge sind dort abgebildet? Schreibe die Zahlen auf. Dann höre zu und überprüfe.

4 What's in the party box?

Number the party decorations in the picture. Then listen and repeat. 35
Nummeriere die Partydekoration im Bild. Dann höre zu und wiederhole.

1. balloons
2. sweets
3. party hats
4. candles
5. garlands

6 A recipe for a party salad

a) Look at the pictures and read the sentences.
Schaue dir die Bilder an und lies die Sätze.

1. Cook the pasta in boiling salted water.

2. Cut the yellow pepper, tomatoes and the zucchini into small pieces.

3. Peel the onion and cut it into small pieces.

4. Mix everything with a large spoon in a bowl.

5. Mix the olive oil, the vinegar, the black pepper and the salt in a cup.

6. Pour the dressing over the pasta and vegetables. Then mix again.

b) Match the English and the German sentences.
Ordne die englischen Sätze den deutschen Sätzen zu.

☐ Schäle die Zwiebel und schneide sie in kleine Stücke.

☐ Dann rühre alles mit einem großen Löffel um.

[1] Koche die Nudeln in kochendem Salzwasser.

☐ Gieße das Dressing über die Nudeln und das Gemüse.

☐ Schneide die gelbe Paprika, Tomaten und die Zucchini in kleine Stücke.

☐ Verrühre das Olivenöl, den Essig, den Pfeffer und das Salz.

8 Looking for a present

a) Look at the picture. Say what you see.
Schaue dir das Bild an. Sag, was du siehst.

b) Listen and read along. 36
Höre zu und lies mit.

Jasmine: This is a great shop. We'll definitely find a good ______________ for Ben.

Sandeep: Yeah, let's have a look around.

Jasmine: Here is some hair gel.
Hm, smells ______________.

Sandeep: Let me see.
No, I think this hair gel here smells better.
Ah, here are some ______________. This green one is cool.

Jasmine: I think this blue cap is cooler than the green one.
And that ______________ one is definitely the coolest.
But is a cap a good present for Ben?

Sandeep: Probably not. We could buy him a ______________.

Jasmine: Well, a voucher is OK. But isn't it much nicer to get Ben a real present?

15 minutes later ...

Sandeep: I'm sure we've found the best present for Ben, much better than a voucher and cheaper than one of the caps.

Jasmine: You're right. Ben loves good ______________ for drawing. Should we get some ______________ for him, too?

Sandeep: Yeah, why not? Or jelly beans.

Jasmine: But let's pay for the pens first. We can buy some ______________ later.

c) Listen again. Complete the text with the words from the box.
Höre noch einmal zu. Vervollständige den Text mit den Wörtern im Kasten.

caps | pens | good | chocolate | present | sweets | black | voucher

9 Presents

Find the words. Finde die Wörter.

Du findest Hilfe bei Aufgabe 8 auf Seite 65.

1. You wear it on your head. c _ _
2. You can write and draw with them. _ _ n s
3. It is usually brown and delicious. c _ _ _ _ _ _ _ _
4. You can buy something nice with it. v _ _ c _ _ _
5. You style your hair with it. h _ _ _ _ _ _
6. They are bad for your teeth. _ _ _ _ t _

10 What's nicer?

a) **What do you think about the presents? Write down at least three sentences.**
Was hältst du von den Geschenken? Schreibe mindestens drei Sätze auf.

The cap is		
The T-shirt is	nicer	
The voucher is	cooler	
The chocolate is	prettier	than the ...
The book is	cheaper	
The sweets are	better	
The pens are		

The chocolate is cheaper than the book.

b) **Compare with a partner.** Vergleicht zu zweit.

13 Good, better, best

a) Which forms belong together? Welche Formen gehören zusammen?

big | funny | good | small | happy |
funnier | happier | smaller | bigger | better |
the happiest | the biggest | the best | the funniest | the smallest

big	bigger	the biggest
______	______	______
______	______	______
______	______	______
______	______	______

b) Complete the sentences with the words from a).
Ergänze die Sätze mit den Wörtern aus a).

(big)
Cake 1 is ______________.
Cake 2 is ______________ than cake 1.
But cake 3 is the ______________.

(small)
Present 1 is ______________.
Present 2 is ______________ than present 1.
But present 3 is the ______________.

(happy)
The boy is ______________.
The girl is ______________ than the boy.
But the dog is the ______________.

18 The surprise party

a) Listen and point at the pictures. 37
Höre zu und zeige auf die Bilder.

1

2

3

4

5

6

☐ When Ben opened the door to the living room, he looked into the faces of his best friends. They were singing "Happy Birthday". The room was decorated with lots of balloons and garlands. What a great surprise!

☐ Afterwards Megan opened the buffet. There were lots of drinks and food: a salad, muffins, crisps, sausages and much more.

☐ They took lots of photos, too. Some of them were really crazy. It was a great surprise party for Ben.

☐ Yesterday Sarah and Ben went to Megan's house. They wanted to watch a film.

☐ Then Sandeep and Josh turned on the music and they all danced. Well, Sir Barks-A-Lot didn't.

☐ Then his friends gave him their presents. He got a comic book, lovely pens for drawing, lots of sweets, a cool T-shirt and a voucher.

b) Read the texts and match them with the pictures.
Lies die Texte und ordne sie den Bildern zu.

c) Copy your favourite part of the story.
Schreibe deinen Lieblingsteil der Geschichte ab.

19 Target task: Your party

a) **Work with a partner. Plan a surprise party for a friend. Circle one or more ideas in the boxes.** Arbeitet zu zweit. Plant eine Überraschungsparty für einen Freund/eine Freundin. Kreist eine oder mehrere Ideen aus den Kästen ein.

Where?

in the garden | in the park | at the lake | at school | at the zoo | ...

When?

in the afternoon | in the evening | at the weekend | on Friday | ...

Decorations?

party hats | balloons | garlands | photos | candles | ...

Things you need?

cake | presents | music | chairs | tables | guests | decorations | ...

Food/drinks?

sweets | crisps | sausages | salad | lemonade | water | juice | vegetables | ...

Activities?

dance | sing | play games | watch videos | swim | ...

b) **Complete the text with your words from a).**
Vervollständigt den Text mit euren Wörtern von a).

A surprise party

We would like to present our party ideas for a surprise party.

The party will be ______.

It will be ______.

We'll have ______.

We'll need ______.

We'll have ______.

We will ______.

c) **Present your party ideas in class.** Stellt eure Partyideen in der Klasse vor.

Theme 5

Dos and don'ts

In diesem *Theme* beschäftigst du dich mit ...

- **Regeln daheim,**
- **Regeln in der Schule,**
- **Schuluniformen.**

1 Problems

a) **Look at the pictures. What are the problems? Tick.**
Schau dir die Bilder an. Welche Probleme gibt es? Mache ein Häkchen.

☐ clothes
☐ being late / going out
☐ untidy rooms
☐ too many computer games
☐ friends

b) **Listen to four dialogues. Number the pictures above.** 38
Höre dir vier Dialoge an. Nummeriere die Bilder oben.

c) How do they feel? Label the pictures with words from the box.
Wie fühlen sie sich? Beschrifte die Bilder mit Wörtern aus der Box.

angry | happy | frustrated | worried | sad | excited

 ____________

 ____________

 ____________

d) How do the parents say the sentences in the pictures? Act it out.
Wie sagen die Eltern die Sätze in den Bildern? Spiele sie nach.

2 Megan and her mum

a) Listen to Megan and her mum. What are they talking about? Tick. 39

Höre Megan und ihrer Mutter zu. Worüber sprechen sie? Mache ein Häkchen.

☐ problems at school ☐ Megan's wishes

b) Read Megan's questions. Find the correct answers.

Lies Megans Fragen. Finde die richtigen Antworten.

1. Mum, can I wear these jeans for Grandma's birthday?
2. May I watch the film at 10 o'clock tomorrow night?
3. Mum, please can I go shopping on Oxford Street after school?
4. Can I have these trainers? They're really cool.
5. Can I go to the youth club with Jasmine?

☐ No, not after school. You can go shopping on Saturday afternoon.

☐ No, you can't. They're too expensive.

☐ Sorry, not the ones with all those holes.

☐ OK, but you have to be back by 8 o'clock.

☐ No, you can't. It's a horror film and it's too late.

c) Read the dialogue in b) with a partner.

Lest den Dialog in b) zu zweit.

3 Talking to Dad

Listen to Megan and her dad. Underline the problems they talk about. 40

Höre Megan und ihrem Vater zu. Unterstreiche die Probleme, über die sie reden.

friends | music | clothes | homework | going out | make-up | pets | money

4 A chat

a) **Read the chat between Jasmine and Sandeep.**
Lies den Chat zwischen Jasmine und Sandeep.

Du kannst dir den Chat auch anhören. 41

b) **How does Jasmine feel? Underline.**
Wie fühlt sich Jasmine? Unterstreiche.

sad | worried | angry | lonely | happy | tired

c) **What are Jasmine's rules at home? Match the sentence parts.**
Wie lauten Jasmines Regeln zu Hause? Ordne die Satzteile einander zu.

1. Jasmine mustn't listen	make-up.
2. Jasmine mustn't wear	be in bed by 9:30.
3. Jasmine has to	to music when she does her homework.

Welche Regeln gibt es bei dir? Versuche, eine auf Englisch zu formulieren.

I mustn't ______________________________.

6 Your rules at home

a) Match the English and the German phrases.
Ordne die englischen und deutschen Ausdrücke einander zu.

1	2	3	4	5
I must … / I have to …	I don't have to …	I mustn't …	I can …	I can't …

☐ ich muss nicht

☐ ich kann, ich darf

☐ ich muss

☐ ich kann nicht, ich darf nicht

☐ ich darf nicht

b) Complete the speech bubbles. Use the phrases from a).
Vervollständige die Sprechblasen. Benutze die Ausdrücke von a).

I ________________ use my phone at mealtimes.

I ________________ wear what I want when I go to school.

I ________________ be in bed by 8 o'clock.

I ________________ take out the rubbish.

I ________________ eat sweets before dinner.

c) Talk about your rules at home with a partner.
Sprecht zu zweit über eure Regeln zu Hause.

I mustn't use my phone at mealtimes. What about you?

8 Rules for Bagheera

a) **What are Jasmine's rules for her cat? Fill in the words.**
Wie lauten Jasmines Regeln für ihre Katze? Füge die Wörter ein.

can (+) has to (!!!) mustn't (⊗)

1. Bagheera (+) ______________________ sleep all day.
2. She (⊗) ______________________ bring home any mice.
3. She (+) ______________________ play with Sir Barks-A-Lot.
4. She (!!!) ______________________ drink enough water every day.
5. She (!!!) ______________________ stay away from the fridge.

b) **What's your favourite pet? What would be the rules for it? Write them down.**
Was ist dein Lieblingshaustier? Welche Regeln würdest du aufstellen? Schreibe sie auf.

Rules for ______________

1 ______________________________

____

2 ______________________________

____

3 ______________________________

____

12 Choose an activity

- **Work in groups. Ask each other about your rules at home. Take notes.**
  Arbeitet in Gruppen. Befragt euch gegenseitig nach euren Regeln daheim. Macht Notizen.

What are your rules at home?

I have to be at home by ...

I mustn't watch TV after ...

name	has to	mustn't
Josef	tidy his room	play too many video games

- **Who says what? Match.**
  Wer sagt was? Ordne zu.

Mum, can I meet my friends in the park now?

No, you can't.

You have to do your homework before you leave.

Please, Mum. We don't have any homework today.

OK, but you have to be back home by 8:30.

Read the dialogue with a partner.
Lest den Dialog zu zweit.

13 Target task: Your role play

a) **Work with a partner. Plan a role play about a problem between children and their parents.** Arbeitet zu zweit. Plant ein Rollenspiel über ein Problem zwischen Kindern und ihren Eltern.

Think of possible problems. Überlegt euch mögliche Probleme.

go out with friends | play video games | wear these jeans | have these trainers | go shopping | watch the film at 10 o'clock | ______

b) **Write a dialogue.** Schreibt einen Dialog.

You can start like this:
So kannst du beginnen:

Can I play video games with my friends?

OK, but first you have to ...

Hilfreiche Redemittel:
You have to ...
No, you can't.
OK, but ...
No, you are too young!

c) **Practise your role play.** Übt euer Rollenspiel.

d) **Act it out.** Spielt es vor.

Überlegt euch, welche Requisiten ihr braucht.

1 Haverstock school rules

a) Listen and read along. 42
Höre zu und lies mit.

HAVERSTOCK SCHOOL RULES

1. Be polite and show respect.
2. School starts at 8:50 a.m. Students who are late must report to the deputy head.
3. Students must not run in the school building.
4. Students must wear school uniform.
5. Students are not allowed to leave the school grounds at break or at lunchtime.
6. Eat and drink in class.
7. Students are not allowed to chew chewing gum.
8. Students are not allowed to use mobile phones.
9. Students must wear sports kit for PE.
10. Put your litter (paper, plastic, …) in the correct bins.

b) Look at the pictures. Which rules are the students breaking?
Schaue dir die Bilder an. Welche Regeln brechen die Schülerinnen und Schüler?

c) Find the rules for these pictures.
Finde die Regeln für diese Bilder.

d) **Read the rules again. Write down what the students must do or are not allowed to do.** Lies die Regeln erneut. Schreibe auf, was die Schülerinnen und Schüler tun müssen oder nicht tun dürfen.

is not allowed to use his mobile phone at school | ~~must report to the deputy head~~ | is not allowed to leave the school grounds at lunchtime | must wear the correct school uniform

1. Ken's alarm clock didn't work. He arrives at school at 9 a.m.

Ken must report to the deputy head.

2. Nasaar wants to wear her new miniskirt at school.

3. Tim wants to call a friend on his mobile phone at lunch.

4. Rosie wants to go home for lunch.

4 Rules at your school

Write down 3 important rules at your school.
Schreibe 3 wichtige Regeln an deiner Schule auf.

1. We must ______.
2. We must not ______.
3. ______.

Here are some ideas:

eat and drink in the classroom | be polite and show respect | wear a cap in the classroom | chew chewing gum at school | wear a school uniform | leave the school grounds at break or lunchtime | skate on school grounds | listen to music | bring a pet to school | ...

5 School cafeteria rules

Schau dir die Mensa-Regeln der Haverstock Schule an.
Beantworte die Fragen von jemandem, der kein Englisch versteht.

Cafeteria Rules

- *Choose a seat and don't run around.*
- *Eat the vegetables, they are not just for decoration.*
- *Talk quietly.*
- *Keep your table and eating area clean.*

Was darf man nicht machen?

Man darf nicht ...

Was soll man machen?

Man soll ...

6 What to wear?

a) What are you wearing at school today? Tick and complete.
Was hast du heute in der Schule an? Mache ein Häkchen und ergänze.

☐	a ______ T-shirt	☐	______ jeans
☐	a ______ shirt	☐	______ trousers
☐	a ______ pullover	☐	a ______ jacket
☐	______ shoes	☐	a ______ cap
☐	______ trainers	☐	a ______ skirt
☐	______ shorts	☐	a ______ dress

b) Talk to a partner. Sprecht zu zweit.

I'm wearing a blue shirt.

c) What must the students at Haverstock School wear? Label the pictures.
Was müssen die Schülerinnen und Schüler an der Haverstock Schule tragen? Beschrifte die Bilder.

grey shirt | black trousers | black shoes | blue pullover | black skirt | blue blazer | tie

d) Talk to a partner. Sprecht zu zweit.

The girls must wear ...

The boys must wear ...

LAND & LEUTE

Schuluniformen

An vielen britischen Schulen tragen Schülerinnen und Schüler eine Schuluniform.
Sie dürfen normalerweise keine Sportschuhe tragen.

An den meisten dieser Schulen gibt es Pullover und Blazer mit dem Abzeichen der Schule.
So kann auf dem Schulweg jeder sofort erkennen, zu welcher Schule man gehört. Es gibt auch keinen Streit über die „richtige“ Jeans- oder Sportschuhmarke oder das coolste Sweatshirt.

Gibt es an deiner Schule Schulkleidung?

9 A uniform for your school

a) **Draw a school uniform for your school.**
Zeichne eine Schuluniform für deine Schule.

Du kannst auch eine Collage machen.

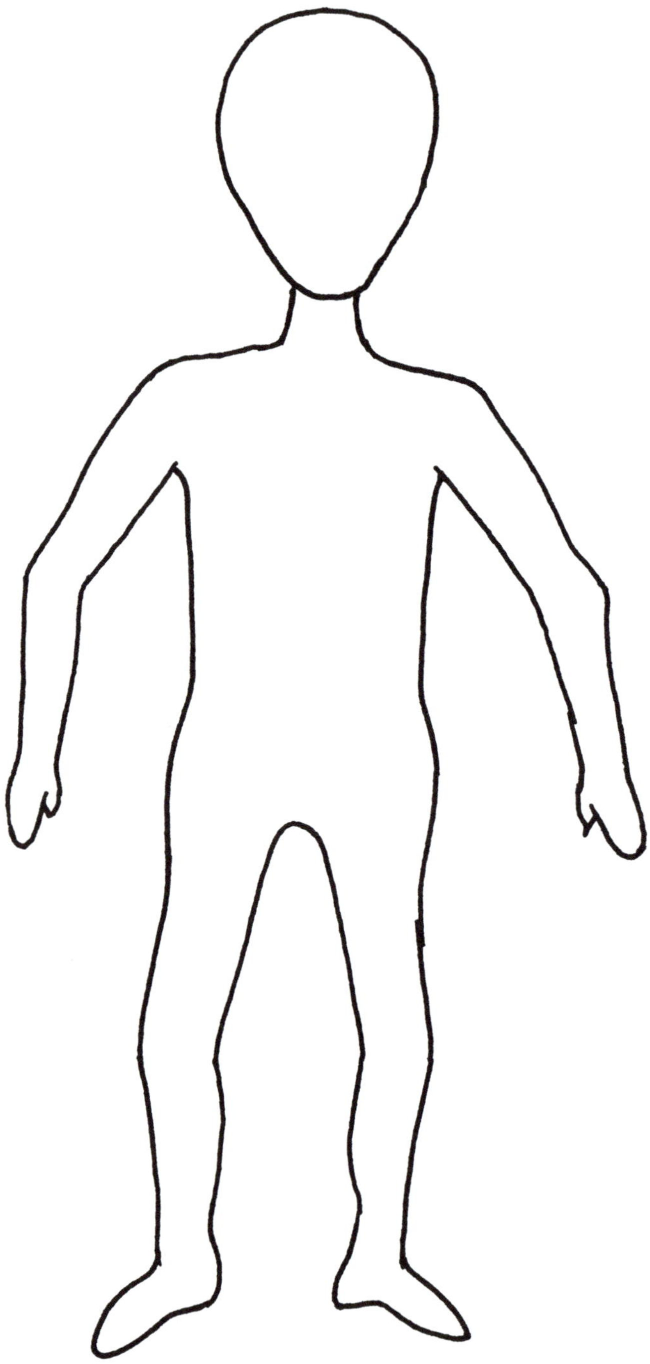

b) **Label your school uniform.** Beschrifte deine Schuluniform.

c) **Present it in class.** Präsentiere sie in der Klasse.

Bei Aufgabe 6 auf Seite 80/81 findest du Hilfe.

10 What is happening?

a) Look at the pictures.
Schau dir die Bilder an.

b) Read the sentences and number them.
Lies die Sätze und nummeriere sie.

> Das englische Wort für Mobbing ist *bullying*.

- ☐ A strong boy is attacking a younger student.
- ☐ Someone is sending a student a threatening text message.
- ☐ A girl is calling a classmate names.
- ☐ A group of girls is saying bad things about another girl.
- ☐ A group of boys is ignoring a classmate.
- ☐ Two boys are taking a classmate's phone.

c) Listen and check. 43
Höre zu und vergleiche.

d) Arbeitet zu zweit. Erklärt euch die Situationen auf Deutsch.

12 Bullying: no chance!

a) What can you do when someone bullies you? Read the tip.
Was kannst du tun, wenn dich jemand mobbt? Lies den Tipp.

Tell your teacher.

b) Find more tips. Make sentences.
Finde mehr Tipps. Bilde Sätze.

I can talk to	from the bullies.
I can write an email to a	with my friends.
I can tell	my friend.
I can stay away	my parents.
I can stay	helpline.

c) Copy the most important tips.
Schreibe die Tipps auf, die dir am wichtigsten sind.

I can ______________________________.

I can ______________________________.

d) Present them in class. Präsentiere sie in der Klasse.

e) Talk about the tips with a partner. Which tip is helpful?
Sprecht zu zweit über die Tipps. Welcher Tipp ist hilfreich?

I would talk ...

I think it is helpful to ...

I wouldn't stay ...

13 Target task: Rules for your class

a) **Work in groups. Make a poster with 4 important rules for your classroom.**
Arbeitet in Gruppen. Macht ein Poster mit 4 wichtigen Regeln für euer Klassenzimmer.

Here are some ideas:
Hier sind einige Ideen:

We must	We must not
be polite to each other.	use our mobile phones.
help each other.	eat in class.
clean our classroom.	forget our homework.
bring our school things.	chew chewing gum.
be quiet.	take things from our classmates.
...	call our classmates names.
	put our feet on the tables.
	...

Rules for our class

b) **Present your poster.** Stellt euer Poster vor.

Theme 6

Let’s go!

In diesem *Theme* beschäftigst du dich mit …

- **Wochenend- und Ferienplänen,**
- **Arztgesprächen,**
- **deinem Lieblingsfernsehprogramm oder deiner Lieblingsserie.**

1 Weekend plans

a) Find the weekend activities. Finde die Wochenendaktivitäten.

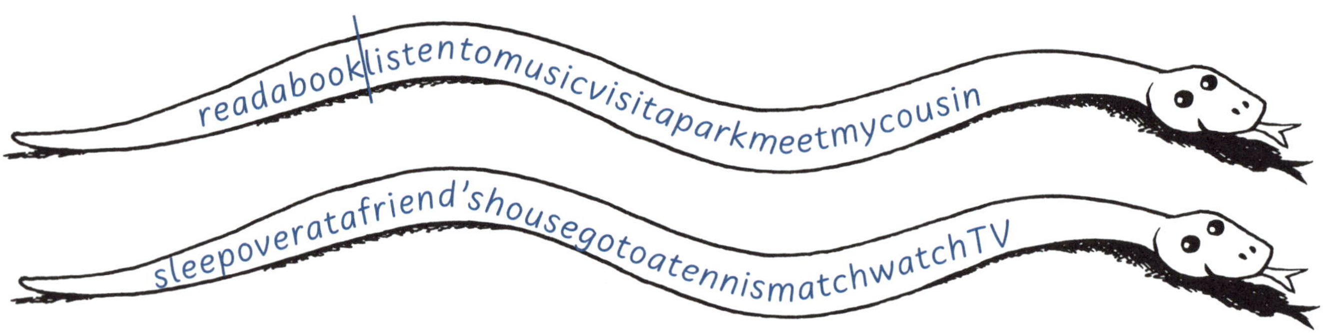

b) Talk to a partner. Sprecht zu zweit.

What are you going to do this weekend?

I’m going to sleep over at a friend’s house.

In den Wortschlangen findest du weitere Ideen.

2 A weekend in Camden

a) Listen and read along. What's wrong with Ben? 44
Höre zu und lies mit. Was ist mit Ben los?

☐ He is ill. ☐ He is tired.

b) Read again. Match the sentence parts.
Lies erneut. Ordne die Satzteile einander zu.

1. Megan has gone	TV.
2. Megan has taken	to a concert.
3. Ben has watched	Sir Barks-A-Lot with her.
4. Jasmine and Jason have gone	to Edinburgh.

3 Visiting a friend

I can see ...

a) **Look at the picture. What can you see?**
Sieh dir das Bild unten an. Was kannst du sehen?

b) **Listen to the dialogue. Underline words you hear.** 45
Höre dir den Dialog an. Unterstreiche Wörter, die du verstanden hast.

Ben | Neela | Sandeep | doctor | book | fruit |
music | homework | school | flowers | card | Sir Barks-A-Lot |
Megan | Jason | Jasmine | chocolate | ill

c) **Listen again and read along.** Höre erneut zu und lies mit.

Sandeep: Hi mate, how are you?
Ben: Still bad. My mum wants to take me to the doctor tomorrow.
Sandeep: I'm sorry, mate. But maybe I can cheer you up. Here's some fruit from our shop. My parents want you to get well soon.
Ben: That's very kind. Please say thank you to them.
Sandeep: And here's something else for you.
Ben: What is it? Homework?
Sandeep: No, it's not. Have a look.
Ben: Oh, it's a card from Megan and Jasmine. How sweet of them.
Sandeep: So what does the card say?
Ben: It says "Cheer up, Ben! We miss you a lot. Love from Megan and Jasmine".
Sandeep: I hope I'll get a card like that next time I'm ill.
Ben: Sure. Jasmine will send you loads of cards.
Sandeep: Ha ha!

4 What are the words?

a) Find the words and write them down.
Finde die Wörter und schreibe sie auf.

doc- | ~~che-~~ | tomorr- | we- | fru- | ca- | ki-	~~-er~~ | -ll | -tor | -it | -nd | -rd | -ow

cheer ______________________

______________________ ______________________

______________________ ______________________

______________________ ______________________

b) Make a quiz for your partner. Use words from the text in number 3.
Mache ein Rätsel für deinen Partner/deine Partnerin. Benutze Wörter aus dem Text in Aufgabe 3.

______________________ ______________________

______________________ ______________________

5 Already done?

What has Ben already done?
What hasn't he done yet? Draw lines.
Was hat Ben schon gemacht?
Was hat er noch nicht gemacht? Verbinde.

- take his medicine ✓
- go to the doctor
- eat fruit
- drink lots of tea and water ✓

1. Ben has already	gone to the doctor yet.
2. Ben hasn't	drunk lots of tea and water.
3. He hasn't	taken his medicine.
4. He has already	eaten fruit yet.

7 At the doctor's

a) Listen and read along. 46
Höre zu und lies mit.

Doctor Clarke: Hello Ben. What's wrong with you?

Ben: Hello Doctor Clarke. I don't feel very well. I have a headache and a sore throat.

Doctor Clarke: Let me see. Well, you don't have a temperature. Now open your mouth, please. OK, your throat is sore. Does it hurt a lot?

Ben: Yes, it does.

Doctor Clarke: Oh dear. It's best to gargle with salt water. And drink lots of warm tea.

Ben: OK, I will.

Doctor Clarke: You can go to school again in two days.

Ben's mum: Thank you, Doctor Clarke.

Doctor Clarke: You're welcome. Goodbye!

Ben and his mum: Goodbye!

Was bedeuten die blauen Wörter im Text? Überlegt zu zweit.

b) Complete the sentences with the words from the box.
Vervollständige die Sätze mit den Wörtern aus dem Kasten.

temperature | headache | gargle | sore throat | throat | sore

1. Ben has a h ___ ___ ___ ___ ___ ___ ___ .
2. He doesn't have a t ___ ___ ___ ___ ___ ___ ___ ___ ___ ___ .
3. But his t ___ ___ ___ ___ ___ hurts. It is s ___ ___ ___ .
4. It is best to drinks lots of warm tea when you have a s ___ ___ ___ t ___ ___ ___ ___ ___ .
5. Or you can g ___ ___ ___ ___ ___ with salt water.

8 What's the problem?

a) Who is at the doctor's? Listen and tick. 47
Wer ist beim Arzt? Höre zu und mache ein Häkchen.

Jasmine

Jasmine's mum

Bagheera

b) Listen again and underline the correct answers.
Höre erneut zu und unterstreiche die richtigen Antworten.

1. Her **hand** **head** hurts.
2. She tripped over her **dog** **cat** and fell.
3. She should **use a cream** **gargle** .

10 What has changed?

Look at the pictures. Make sentences. Use the words from the box.
Schau dir die Bilder an. Bilde Sätze. Benutze die Wörter aus dem Kasten.

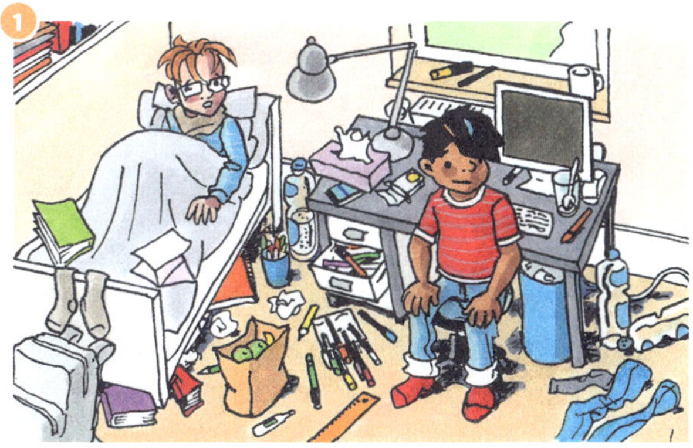

1. Ben has made ______.
2. He has cleaned ______.
3. He has tidied ______.
4. He has put away ______.

his floor
his pencils
his desk
his bed

12 What to watch?

a) Match the words with the pictures.
Ordne die Wörter den Bildern zu.

1. a soap opera | 2. a talk show | 3. a film | 4. a talent show | 5. a quiz show | 6. a sports programme | 7. the news | 8. a cartoon

b) Talk to a partner. What kind of programmes do you like?
Sprecht zu zweit. Welche Sendungen magst du?

I like ...

I always watch ...

I sometimes watch ...

I never watch ...

13 Watching TV

Lies dir Bens Blogeintrag über seine Fernsehgewohnheiten durch. Beantworte die Fragen von jemandem, der kaum Englisch versteht.

I usually watch TV when I'm ill. My favourite TV programme is Ackley Bridge. It's on Channel 4 and it's a kind of soap. It's about students and teachers at a school in the north of England.
I like watching Ackley Bridge because it's exciting but also very funny.

1. Wann schaut Ben fern?
2. Wo kann man Bens Lieblingssendung sehen?
3. Was für eine Sendung ist es?

Du kannst erst die englischen Antworten im Text unterstreichen.

LAND & LEUTE

Fernsehen in Großbritannien

In Großbritannien gibt es ein großes Angebot an Fernsehsendern. Dazu gehören die beiden werbefreien Sender *BBC1* und *BBC2*. Mit Begeisterung sehen sich Jugendliche in Großbritannien Castingshows an.
Aber auch in Großbritannien schauen immer mehr junge Leute Filme und Serien auf ihrem Mobiltelefon, Laptop oder Tablet und nicht auf dem Fernsehgerät.

Welche Geräte nutzt du, um dir Filme oder Serien anzuschauen?
Wie heißt deine Lieblingssendung oder Lieblingsserie?

14 Target task: Your favourite programme or series

a) **Make a poster about your favourite programme or series with words or sentences.** Erstelle ein Poster über deine Lieblingssendung oder Lieblingsserie mit Wörtern oder Sätzen.

My favourite programme or series

Favourite programme or series? ______________________

Kind of programme or series? ______________________

Channel? ______________________

Day? ______________________

Time? ______________________

How? ______________________

Where? ______________________

What is it like? ______________________

b) **Present your poster in class.** Präsentiere dein Poster in der Klasse.

1 Have you ever ...?

a) Listen to the song and sing along. 48
Höre dir das Lied an und sing mit.

Have you ever been to Paris? ___
Have you ever been to Rome? ___
Have you ever been to London? ___
No, I've just been here at home. ___

Have you ever met a stunt man? ___
Have you ever met the Queen? ___
Have you ever met a T. Rex? ___
No, I've just seen them on screen. ___

b) Look at the pictures. Match them with the song lines.
Schau dir die Bilder an. Ordne sie den Liedzeilen zu.

1 
2 
3 
4 
5 
6 
7 
8 

c) Talk to a partner. Sprecht zu zweit.

Have you ever been to Paris?

Yes, I have.

No, I haven't.

2 Choose an activity

- **Work with a partner. Practise the song in number 1 and present it in class. You can also record it.** Arbeitet zu zweit. Übt das Lied von Aufgabe 1 und präsentiert es in der Klasse. Ihr könnt es auch aufnehmen.
- **Number the flags. Then listen and repeat.** 49
  Nummeriere die Flaggen. Dann höre zu und sprich nach.

 ☐
 ☐
 ☐
 ☐
 ☐

1. Denmark
2. Spain
3. Germany
4. Great Britain
5. Austria

3 Holiday plans

a) **Look at the picture. Who is in the garden? Talk to a partner.**
Schau dir das Bild an. Wer ist im Garten? Sprecht zu zweit.

b) **Listen to Megan and her friends. What's their plan for the holidays? Tick.** 50
Höre Megan und ihren Freunden zu. Was ist ihr Plan für die Ferien? Mache ein Häkchen.

☐ a party ☐ a holiday camp

c) **Listen again. Match the sentences with the pictures.**
Höre erneut zu. Ordne die Sätze den Bildern zu.

... has never been to Cornwall.

... wants to eat ice cream every day.

... is looking forward to the sea.

... is interested in visiting castles.

5 More questions

Put the questions in the right order. Bringe die Fragen in die richtige Reihenfolge.

1. Have – already done – your homework – you – ?

____

2. Have – ever been – you – to a concert – ?

____

3. Have – already tidied – your room – you – ?

____

6 Holidays in Cornwall

a) **Look at the title of the brochure and the picture. What is it about?**
Schau dir den Titel der Broschüre und das Bild an. Worum geht es?

☐ an adventure camp ☐ a swimming course

b) **Read the brochure.** Lies die Broschüre.

Cornish Adventure Camp
for young people from 8 to 16

There is never a boring moment at the Cornish Adventure Camp in Newquay.

Newquay has some of the best beaches in the UK. We do lots of fun activities at the beach, like bodyboarding and surfing.
We also go on a treasure hunt.

What's more, you can come with us to Blue Reef Newquay. It's an amazing aquarium with an underwater tunnel.

And we visit Tintagel Castle.

So don't miss out. Spend your holidays at the Cornish Adventure Camp!

c) **Read the questions. Mark the answers in the text.**
Lies die Fragen. Markiere die Antworten im Text.

Für welche Altersgruppe ist das Ferienlager?

Wo ist das Ferienlager?

Welche Aktivitäten werden am Strand angeboten?

Welche Ausflüge werden angeboten?

d) **Sprecht zu zweit. Was habt ihr noch verstanden?**

8 What do they need?

a) **Fill in the crossword.** Fülle das Kreuzworträtsel aus.

money | book | cap | sweets | torch | swimwear | phone

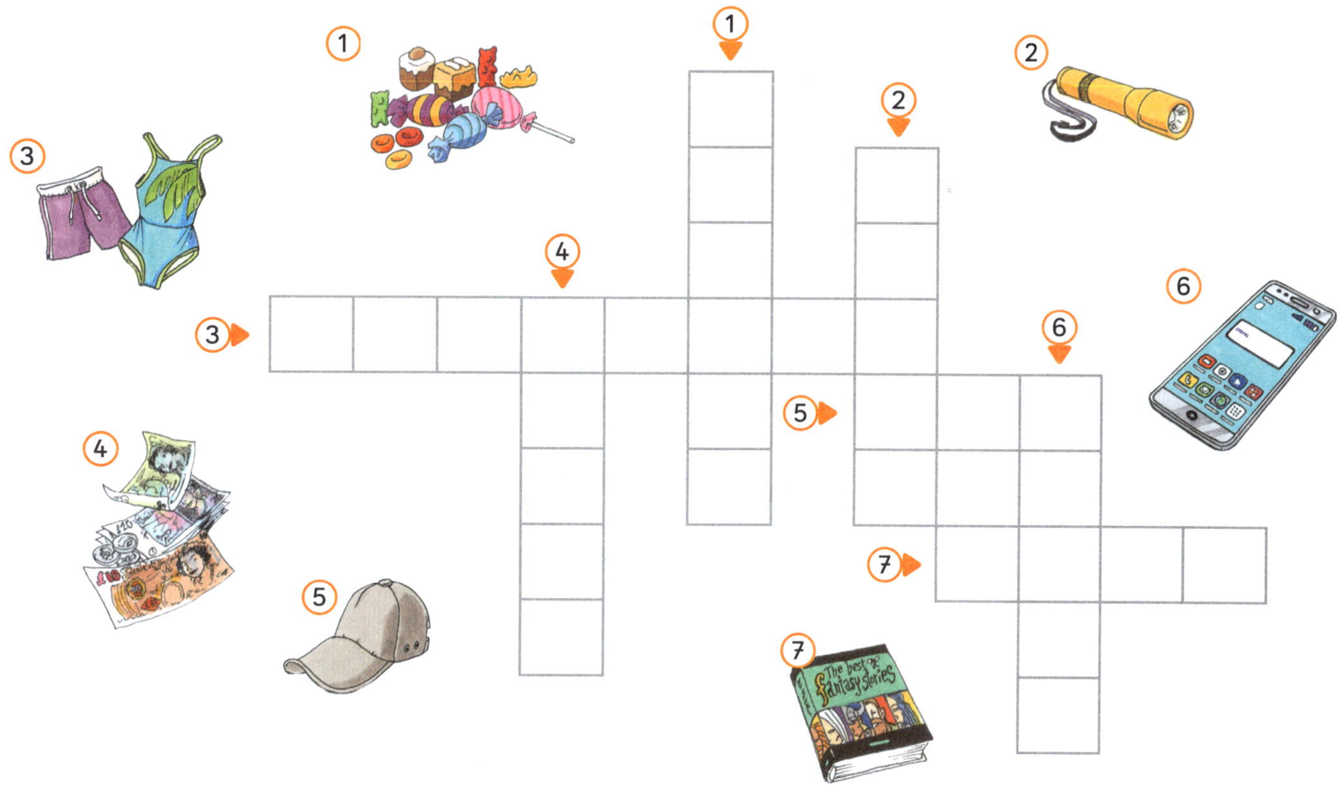

b) **What would you pack for a summer holiday? Write it down.**
Was würdest du für deinen Sommerurlaub einpacken? Schreibe es auf.

sunglasses ☑
________ ☐
________ ☐
________ ☐
________ ☐

sunglasses

flip-flops

sun cream

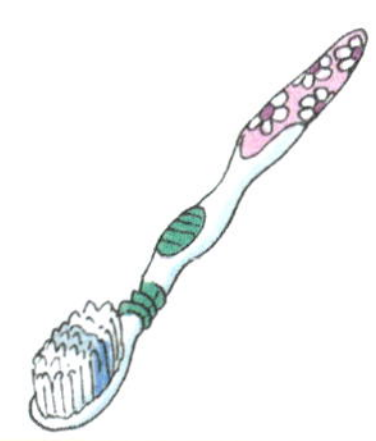
toothbrush

c) **Talk to a partner.** Sprecht zu zweit.

I would pack ...

9 On the beach in Cornwall

a) **Look at the pictures. Say what you see.**
Schau dir die Bilder an. Sag, was du siehst.

b) **Read the story.** Lies die Geschichte.

A The four friends were on the beach in Newquay. They learned how to bodyboard.

B Megan, Sandeep and Jasmine jumped into the waves. But Ben stayed on the beach.

C Sandeep noticed that Ben was missing. They called his name and started looking for him. They got really worried.

D The friends found Ben again. He was drawing pictures in his sketchbook.

c) **Listen. Then match the speech bubbles and the pictures.** 51
Höre zu. Dann ordne die Sprechblasen den Bildern zu.

1. Ben! Where are you?

2. Oh, there's a big wave. Let's go and catch it.

3. Oh, hi guys. Sorry, I didn't feel like bodyboarding. I drew a picture of you.

4. I can't. My body hurts from our trip to the castle yesterday.

d) **Read the story again. Then complete the sentences. Use the words from the box.** Lies die Geschichte erneut. Dann vervollständige die Sätze. Benutze die Wörter aus dem Kasten.

worried | bodyboards | missing | looked | waves | water | pictures

1. The friends were on the beach with their b __ __ __ __ __ __ __ __ __.
2. Then they took their boards to the w __ __ __ __.
3. They jumped into the w __ __ __ __.
4. Sandeep noticed that Ben was m __ __ __ __ __ __.
5. The friends were w __ __ __ __ __ __ and l __ __ __ __ __ for Ben.
6. Then they found him. He was drawing p __ __ __ __ __ __ __.

10 A holiday dialogue

a) **Listen and read along.** 52
Höre zu und lies mit.

Felix: Hi, I'm Felix. What's your name?
Sandeep: Hi, my name is Sandeep.
Where are you from?
Felix: I'm from Stuttgart in Germany.
What about you?
Sandeep: I'm from London.
Why don't we play some beach volleyball?
Felix: Yeah, good idea.
Sandeep: I need to put on a shirt and a cap first.
Felix: No problem. See you.
Sandeep: See you.

b) **Complete the dialogue. Work with a partner. Then present it in class.**
Vervollständigt den Dialog. Arbeitet zu zweit. Dann präsentiert ihn vor der Klasse.

A: Hi, I'm ______________________. What's your name?
B: Hi, my name is ______________________.
Where are you from?
A: I'm from ______________ in ______________.
What about you?
B: I'm from ______________________.
Why don't we ______________________?
A: Yeah, good idea.
B: I need to ______________________ first.
A: No problem. See you.
B: See you.

go swimming
build sandcastles
have an ice cream
play football
go bodyboarding
go surfing
...

ask my parents
drink something
get my board
...

12 Target task: Your holiday plans

a) **Work with a partner or on your own. Collect ideas.**
Arbeite mit einem Partner/einer Partnerin oder alleine. Sammle Ideen.

Where would you like to go?
Spain, Denmark, Berlin, ...

How can you get there?
by car, by plane, by train, by boat ...

What can you do there?
go swimming, visit a park, go riding, play football, go shopping, ...

What should you take with you?
sunglasses, swimwear, money, toothbrush, ...

b) **Make a poster for a presentation. Add pictures, words and short sentences.**
Erstelle ein Poster für eine Präsentation. Füge Bilder, Wörter und kurze Sätze hinzu.

My holiday plans

c) **Present your poster.** Präsentiere dein Poster.

Theme 1 After the holidays

Complete the wordbank. Vervollständige die Wortfelder.

Wörter, um über das Wetter zu sprechen:

(→ Seite 7, 9, 14-15)

• windy

Wörter und Sätze, um zu sagen, was du in den Ferien gemacht hast:

(→ Seite 6-7, 9-11, 14-15)

• I visited

Wörter, um deine Ferien zu beschreiben:

(→ Seite 7, 15)

• great

Wörter, die mit der Schule zu tun haben:

(→ Seite 16-18, 21)

• library, maths, uniform

Theme 2 Around London

Complete the wordbank. Vervollständige die Wortfelder.

Aktivitäten in London: (→ Seite 23-24)

- listen to Big Ben

Wörter und Sätze, um den Weg zu beschreiben: (→ Seite 32-33)

- turn left

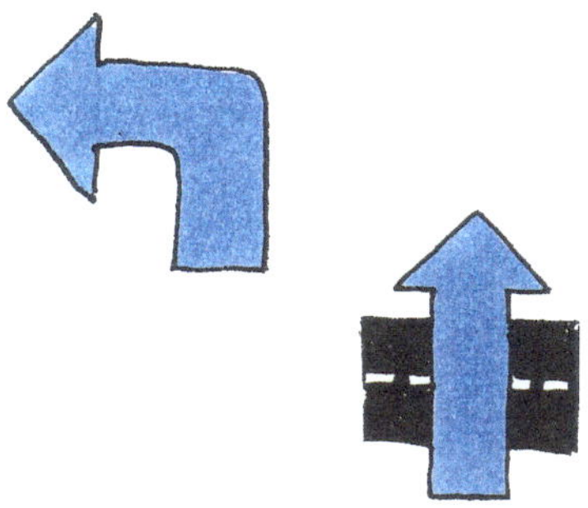

Tiere: (→ Seite 34-35)

- gorilla

Wörter, um Tiere zu beschreiben: (→ Seite 35, 37)

- small

Theme 3 Dreams

Complete the wordbank. Vervollständige die Wortfelder.

Wörter und Sätze, um über deine Zukunft zu sprechen: (→ Seite 40-42, 45)

- I will have a good job.

Berufe: (→ Seite 43-44)

- shop assistant

Wörter und Sätze, um zu beschreiben, wie jemand etwas macht: (→ Seite 51-52)

- They sing loudly.

Theme 4 Celebrations

Complete the wordbank. Vervollständige die Wortfelder.

Feste:

(→ Seite 54-56)

- Christmas

Aktivitäten bei Festen:

(→ Seite 57, 59-61, 69)

- decorate the room

Dinge für eine Party:

(→ Seite 62-63, 69)

- a packet of crisps, garlands

Theme 5 Dos and don'ts

Complete the wordbank. Vervollständige die Wortfelder.

Gefühle: (→ Seite 71, 73)

• happy

Worüber man zu Hause streitet: (→ Seite 70, 72)

• make-up

Regeln: (→ Seite 74-76, 78-79, 85)

• I must wear a school uniform.

Schuluniform: (→ Seite 81-82)

• tie

Theme 6 Let's go!

Complete the wordbank. Vervollständige die Wortfelder.

Wochenendaktivitäten: (→ Seite 86-87)

- visit a park

Beim Arzt: (→ Seite 90-91)

- gargle

Fernsehsendungen und Serien: (→ Seite 92-93)

- a talent show

Dinge, die man im Urlaub braucht: (→ Seite 97, 101)

- sunglasses

Auf den folgenden Seiten kannst du noch einmal nachschlagen, wie du etwas auf Englisch sagen kannst.

1 So kannst du über dich selbst Auskunft geben:

My name is Jasmine.

I am twelve years old. / **I'm** twelve years old.

I am from Leeds. / **I'm** from Leeds.

2 So kannst du über eine andere Person Auskunft geben:

His name is Sandeep.

He is from England.

His hobby is football.

He **has got** brown eyes.

He **hates** baked beans.

Her name is Megan.

She is twelve years old.

Her hobby is dancing.

She **likes** orange juice.

She **plays** rugby.

3 So sagst du, ob du etwas hast oder besitzt:

I **have got** a dog. / I**'ve got** a dog.

I **haven't got** a pencil.

4 So fragst du, ob jemand etwas hat:

Have you **got** a ruler?

5 So kannst du beschreiben, was es (irgendwo) gibt:

There is a chair.

There are two chairs.

6 So sagst du, wem (oder zu wem) etwas gehört:

Megan**'s** birthday is in May.

Ben**'s** budgies are green and yellow.

Jasmine**'s** brother is called Jason.

7 So sagst du, ob du etwas magst:

☺ I **like** jam.

☹ I **don't like** cheese.

8 So fragst du, ob jemand etwas mag:

Do you **like** tennis? – Yes, I do. / No, I don't.

9 So sprichst du von mehreren Dingen oder Personen:

1 girl  → 2 girl**s** 

1 football  → 2 football**s** 

10 So sagst du, wo genau sich etwas befindet:

The smiley is **on** the box. 

The smiley is **under** the box. 

The smiley is **next to** the box. 

The smiley is **in front of** the box. 

11 So sagst du, wie häufig du etwas tust.

I **always** take out the rubbish.

I **often** lay the table.

I **sometimes** tidy my room.

I **never** make my bed.

12 So sagst du, ob du etwas tun kannst:

I **can play** the guitar.

I **can't play** tennis.

13 So sagst du, was du gerade (in diesem Moment) tust:

I **am playing** football. / I'**m playing** football.

14 So sagst du, was andere gerade tun:

Jason **is listening** to music.

The boys **are playing** football.

15 So kannst du sagen, was schon passiert ist (zum Beispiel gestern, letzte Woche oder letztes Jahr):

My grandma **played** video games **yesterday**.

Jasmine **was** in Leeds **last week**.

I **went** to France **last year**.

Wenn etwas nicht passiert ist, sagst du:

I **didn't** play basketball.

He **didn't** go to the cinema.

Fragen stellst du so:

Did you **go** to the beach yesterday? – Yes, I did. / No, I didn't.

What **did** you **do** yesterday? – I went to a party.

16 So vergleichst du Sachen, Tiere und Personen miteinander:

The dog is **small**.

The cat is **smaller**.

The mouse is **the smallest**.

An elephant is **bigger than** a dog.

17 So kannst du sagen, was in der Zukunft passieren wird:

I **will** have a good job in twenty years.

So kürzt du *will* ab:

I'**ll** have a wife and two children.

Wenn etwas nicht passieren wird, sagst du:

I **won't** live in London.

She **won't** be famous.

18 So kannst du ausdrücken, wie man etwas macht:

He sings **loudly**.

The cow is running **fast**.

The dog barks **angrily**.

19 So sagst du, dass jemand etwas tun muss oder nicht tun darf:

Ben **must** tidy his room.

I **must** go to school.

You **mustn't** eat too much chocolate.

I **mustn't** steal Jasmine's lunchbox.

20 So sagst du, ob jemand schon etwas getan hat:

I **have already decorated** the room.

They **have already done** the shopping.

He **hasn't done** his homework **yet**.

A		
a/an	ein(e)	**a** dog / **an** animal
a few	einige	
a lot (of)	viel(e); sehr	
about	über; an	
above	oben	
abroad	im Ausland	
access	Zugang	
acrobat	Akrobat/in	
act	schauspielern	
act out	nachspielen	
activity	Aktivität	1 **activity** – 2 activities
add	hinzufügen	
adventure	Abenteuer, Erlebnis	
after	nach	
in the afternoon	am Nachmittag, nachmittags	
this afternoon	heute Nachmittag	
afterwards	danach; später	
again	wieder, noch (ein)mal	Read the text **again**. – Lies den Text noch einmal.
(three years) ago	vor (drei Jahren)	
alarm clock	Wecker	
all	alle(s)	
all day	den ganzen Tag	
all kinds of	alle möglichen	
along	am ... entlang	
already	schon	
also	auch	
always	immer	
a.m.	morgens, vormittags	9 **a.m.** – 9 Uhr morgens
amazing	toll, unglaublich	
and	und	
angry	verärgert; zornig; wütend	
animal	Tier	
annoying	nervig, lästig	
another	noch ein(e, r, s); ein anderer/anderes, eine andere	
answer	Antwort	
answer	antworten	
any	irgendwelche, irgendein(e)	
not any	kein(e)	
anyone	jede/r; (irgend)jemand	I **am** – ich bin
anywhere	irgendwo	you **are** – du bist
are	bist, sind, seid; kosten	he / she / it **is** – er / sie / es ist
around	um; in; herum, umher	we **are** – wir sind
arrive	ankommen	you **are** – ihr seid
art	Kunst	they **are** – sie sind

Asia	Asien	
ask	fragen; bitten	
at	auf, an, in, bei	
ate	Vergangenheitsform von „eat“	He **ate** a banana. – Er hat eine Banane gegessen.
at a time	auf einmal	
at least	mindestens, wenigstens	
attack	angreifen	
Australia	Australien	
Austria	Österreich	
away	weg	
aww	ach, ah, oh	

B		
back	Rücken; Rückseite	
back	zurück	
bad	schlecht	
balloon	Ballon	
banana	Banane	
barbecue	Grillparty; Grill	
bark	bellen	The dog **barks** loudly. – Der Hund bellt laut.
be	sein	
be about	handeln von	
be allowed	dürfen	
beach	Strand	
beautiful	schön	
most beautiful	schönste(r, s)	
beautifully	schön	
because	weil	
become	werden	
bed	Bett	
been	siehe „be“	I have **been** to London. – Ich bin schon mal in London gewesen.
before	vor; bevor	
beginning	Anfang	
believe (in)	glauben (an)	
belong (to)	gehören (zu)	
best	beste(r, s); am meisten/ liebsten/besten	
better	besser; lieber, mehr	
between	zwischen	
big	groß	
bigger	größer	
biggest	größte(r, s)	
bike	(Fahr)rad	
bin	Mülleimer, Mülltonne	
birthday	Geburtstag	
birthday party	Geburtstagsparty	My **birthday party** is on Friday. – Meine Geburtstagsparty findet am Freitag statt.
black	schwarz	

blazer	Blazer, Jacke	
blind date	Blinddate; Verabredung mit einem/einer Unbekannten	
blue	blau	
boat	Boot; Schiff	
body	Körper	
bodyboarding	Bodyboarden	
boiling	kochend	**boiling** water – kochendes Wasser
book	Buch	
boring	langweilig	
borrow	leihen	
borrowing	(Aus)leihen	
bottle	Flasche	
bowl	Schüssel	
boy	Junge	
break	Pause	We play football at **break**. – Wir spielen in der Pause Fuβball.
break	(zer)brechen	
bricklayer	Maurer/in	
bridge	Brücke	
brilliant	toll, hervorragend, klasse	
bring	(mit)bringen	
brochure	Broschüre	
brother	Bruder	
brought	Vergangenheitsform von „bring“	They **brought** the people home. – Sie brachten die Leute nach Hause.
brown	braun	
build	bauen	
building	Gebäude	
bully	Person, die andere mobbt	
bully	tyrannisieren, mobben	
bullying	Mobbing	
bus driver	Busfahrer/in	
but	aber	
buy	kaufen	
by	bei, in der Nähe; mit, durch	
by (bus)	mit (dem Bus)	I go to school **by bus**. – Ich fahre mit dem Bus zur Schule.
by (eight o'clock)	(spätestens) bis (acht Uhr)	
bye for now	bis bald	

C

cake	Kuchen	
call	(an)rufen; nennen	
call sb names	jdn beschimpfen	
came	Vergangenheitsform von „come“	He **came** with us. – Er kam mit.
campsite	Campingplatz, Zeltplatz	

can	können	**Can** you help me, please? – Kannst du mir bitte helfen?
can't (= cannot)	nicht können	
candle	Kerze	
cap	Mütze, Kappe	
car	Auto	
card	Karte	
careful	vorsichtig; sorgfältig	Be **careful**! – Sei vorsichtig!
carefully	vorsichtig	
carrot	Möhre, Karotte, Mohrrübe	
castle	Burg; Schloss	
cat	Katze	
catch	fangen; erwischen, kriegen	
celebrate	feiern	
celebration	Feier, Fest	
chair	Stuhl	1 **chair** – 2 chairs
change	sich verändern	
channel	Kanal, Programm	
cheap	billig, preiswert	
check	überprüfen, kontrollieren	
cheer	jubeln	
cheer sb up	jdn aufmuntern	
Cheer up!	Lass (doch) den Kopf nicht hängen!, Kopf hoch!	
chess	Schach(spiel)	We played **chess** yesterday. – Wir haben gestern Schach gespielt.
chew	kauen	
chewing gum	Kaugummi	
child/children	Kind/Kinder	
Chinese New Year	Chinesisches Neujahr	
chocolate	Schokolade	
choose	auswählen	
Christmas	Weihnachten	
church	Kirche	
cinema	Kino	
circle	einkreisen, umkringeln	**Circle** the right answer. – Kreise die richtige Antwort ein.
city	(Groß)stadt	
class	(Schul)klasse	
classmate	Klassenkamerad/in, Mitschüler/in	
classroom	Klassenzimmer	
clean	sauber machen, reinigen, putzen	I **cleaned** the kitchen. – Ich habe die Küche geputzt.
clean	sauber	
clever	klug, gescheit, schlau	
climb	klettern	
clock	Uhr	
clothes	Kleider, Kleidung	
cloud	Wolke	

cloudy	bewölkt, bedeckt	
club	Klub, Verein; AG	
coke	Cola	
cold	kalt	
collect	sammeln	
colour	Farbe	My favourite **colour** is yellow. – Meine Lieblingsfarbe ist Gelb.
come	kommen	
come in	hereinkommen	
come to sb's mind	jdm einfallen	
come up	bevorstehen, kommen	
compare	vergleichen	
complete	vervollständigen, ergänzen	**Complete** the sentences. – Vervollständige die Sätze.
computer game	Computerspiel	
concert	Konzert	
cook	kochen	
copy	abschreiben; aufschreiben	
Cornish	kornisch, aus Cornwall	
correct	richtig, korrekt	
costume	Tracht, Kostüm	
could	Vergangenheitsform von „can"; könnte(st, n, t)	We **could** go to the park. – Wir könnten in den Park gehen.
course	Kurs	
cover	bedecken	
crazy	verrückt	
cream	Sahne; Creme	
crisps	Chips	
cross	überqueren	
crossword	Kreuzworträtsel	
cucumber	(Salat)gurke	Cut the **cucumber**. – Schneide die Gurke.
cup	Tasse	
cut	schneiden	
cycling	Radfahren, Radeln	

D

dad	Papa, Vati	
damn	verdammt	
dance	tanzen	
dangerous	gefährlich	
dangerously	gefährlich	
dark	dunkel	
daughter	Tochter	I am my mother's **daughter**. – Ich bin die Tochter meiner Mutter.
day	Tag	
day out	Ausflug	
dead	tot; leer	
dear	liebe(r) *(Anrede)*	
December	Dezember	
decorate	dekorieren, schmücken	

decoration	Dekoration, Schmuck	
definitely	eindeutig, definitiv	
delicious	köstlich, lecker	This cake is **delicious**! – Dieser Kuchen ist lecker!
Denmark	Dänemark	
deputy head	stellvertretende/r Schulleiter/in, Konrektor/in	
describe	beschreiben	
design	entwerfen	
desk	Schreibtisch	
dialogue	Dialog, Gespräch	
diary	Tagebuch	
did	Vergangenheitsform von „do“	I **did** my homework at 4 o'clock. – Ich habe meine Hausaufgaben um 16 Uhr gemacht.
didn't (= did not)	Vergangenheitsform von „do not“	
different	anders; verschieden	
dinner	Abendessen; Mittagessen	
direction	Richtung	
give directions	den Weg beschreiben	
Diwali	hinduistisches Lichterfest	
do	machen, tun	
doctor	Arzt/Ärztin	
does	er/sie/es macht	
doesn't (= does not)	er/sie/es macht nicht	She **doesn't** play tennis. – Sie spielt kein Tennis.
dog	Hund	
dolphin	Delfin	
don't (= do not)	ich mache nicht; du machst nicht; wir/sie machen nicht; ihr macht nicht	
Don't worry!	Keine Sorge!; Keine Angst!	
done	gemacht; fertig, erledigt	
done	siehe „do“	I have **done** my homework. – Ich habe meine Hausaufgaben gemacht.
door	Tür	
dos and don'ts	was man tun und was man nicht tun sollte	
dramatic	dramatisch	
draw	zeichnen	
draw a line	eine Linie ziehen	
drawing	Zeichnen; Zeichnung	
dream	Traum	my **dream** classroom – mein Traumklassenzimmer
dress	Kleid	
dress up (as)	sich verkleiden (als)	
drink	Getränk	
drink	trinken	
drive	fahren	

drummer	Trommler/in; Schlagzeuger/in	
drunk	siehe „drink“	He has **drunk** his tea. – Er hat seinen Tee getrunken.
during	während	

E

each	jede(r, s)	
each other	einander	
ear	Ohr	
Easter	Ostern, das Osterfest	
eat	essen	
eaten	siehe „eat“	I have **eaten** three apples. – Ich habe drei Äpfel gegessen.
eating area	Essbereich; Speiseraum	
egg	Ei	
Eid	islamisches Fest zum Abschluss des Fastenmonats Ramadan	
elephant	Elefant	
end	Ende	
ending	Ende, Schluss	
English	Englisch; englisch	
enjoy	mögen; genießen	
enough	genug	
entry	Eintrag	
in the evening	am Abend, abends	We play video games **in the evening**. – Wir spielen abends Videospiele.
ever	jemals	
every	jede(r, s)	
everyone	jede(r); alle	
everything	alles	
exactly	genau	
example	Beispiel	for **example** – zum Beispiel
excited	aufgeregt	
exciting	aufregend; spannend	
Excuse me!	Entschuldigen Sie bitte!, Entschuldigung!	
expensive	teuer	

F

face	Gesicht	
fact file	Steckbrief	
fall in love (with)	sich verlieben (in)	
fall	fallen	
family	Familie	
famous	berühmt	
fantastic	fantastisch, wunderbar	
farm	Bauernhof	
fast	schnell	The dog ran very **fast**. – Der Hund rannte sehr schnell.
father	Vater	

favourite	Lieblings-	
February	Februar	
feel	(sich) fühlen	
festival	Fest; Festival	We danced at the **festival**. – Wir haben auf dem Fest getanzt.
fill in	ausfüllen, eintragen	
filtered	gefiltert	
find	finden	
fine	in Ordnung, gut	
fireworks	Feuerwerk	
first	zuerst, als Erstes; erste(r, s)	
fish	Fisch(e)	1 **fish** – 2 fish
flag	Fahne, Flagge	
flip flops	Badelatschen	
floor	Boden	
flower	Blume	
fly	fliegen	
folder	Mappe, Schnellhefter	
follow	folgen	**Follow** me! – Folge mir!
food	Essen; Nahrung, Futter	
foot/feet	Fuß/Füße	
football	Fußball	
football player	Fußballspieler/in	
for	für	
forever	ewig	
forget	vergessen	She **forgot** her phone. – She hat ihr Handy vergessen.
forgot	Vergangenheitsform von „forget“	
found	Vergangenheitsform von „find“	They **found** Ben. – Sie haben Ben gefunden.
France	Frankreich	
French	Französisch; französisch	
fresh	frisch	
Friday	Freitag	
fridge	Kühlschrank	
friend	Freund/in	
friendly	freundlich	
frog	Frosch	
from	von, aus	
fruit	Frucht; Obst	An apple is a **fruit**. – Ein Apfel ist eine Frucht.
frustrated	frustriert; enttäuscht	
fun	Spaß, lustig, witzig, spaßig	
funniest	lustigste(r, s)	
funny	lustig, witzig, komisch	
fur	Fell; Pelz	
future	Zukunft	

G		
game	Spiel	
garage	Garage; Werkstatt	
garden	Garten	
gargle	gurgeln	
garland	Girlande	
gave	Vergangenheitsform von „give“	He **gave** me a present. – Er gab mir ein Geschenk.
German	Deutsch; deutsch	
Germany	Deutschland	
get	besorgen; bekommen; hinkommen; holen; werden	
get off	aussteigen	
get started (on)	beginnen (mit)	
get well	gesund werden	Get well soon! – Gute Besserung!
girl	Mädchen	
give	geben; fahren	
go bodyboarding	bodyboarden gehen	
go for a ride	rumfahren, eine Fahrt machen	
go	gehen; fahren	
go abroad	ins Ausland reisen	
go on	weitergehen; weitermachen	
go out	hinausgehen, hinausfahren; ausgehen	
go riding	reiten	
go shopping	einkaufen gehen	I **went shopping** on Saturday. – Ich bin am Samstag einkaufen gegangen.
go surfing	surfen gehen	
go swimming	schwimmen gehen	
goal	Tor	
going to	werden	
gone	siehe „go“	She has **gone** to Berlin. – Sie ist nach Berlin gefahren.
good	gut	
good-looking	gut aussehend	
good-luck	Glücks-	
goodbye	auf Wiedersehen	
got	Vergangenheitsform von „get“	He **got** a nice shirt. – Er bekam ein schönes Hemd.
grandma	Oma, Omi	
grandparents	Großeltern	
grass	Gras; Wiese, Rasen	
great	großartig, toll	
Great Britain	Großbritannien	
green	grün	
grey	grau	
group	Gruppe	Work in **groups**. – Arbeitet in Gruppen.

guard	Wache	
guess	(er)raten	
guest	Gast	
guide	Führer/in	
guinea pig	Meerschweinchen	
guitar	Gitarre	
guys	Leute	
gym (= gymnasium)	Turnhalle, Fitnessstudio	

H

had	Vergangenheitsform von „have“	I **had** a great day. – Ich hatte einen tollen Tag.
hair	Haar, Haare	
hair clip	Haarclip; Haarspange	
hair gel	Haargel	
hairdresser	Friseur/in	
half brother	Halbbruder	Adam is my **half brother**. – Adam ist mein Halbbruder.
Hanukkah	jüdisches Lichterfest	
happen	geschehen, passieren	
happily	glücklich; zufrieden; fröhlich	
happy	glücklich; zufrieden; fröhlich	
Happy Birthday!	Alles Gute zum Geburtstag!	
hard	hart; schwer	
hat	Hut; Mütze	I **have got** – ich habe you **have got** – du hast he/she/it **has got** – er/sie/es hat we **have got** – wir haben you **have got** – ihr habt they **have got** – sie haben
have	haben; essen	
have a barbecue	grillen, eine Grillparty feiern	
have a look (at)	(sich) (an)schauen	
have a meal	eine Mahlzeit zu sich nehmen	
have a party	eine Party feiern	
have a picnic	ein Picknick machen; picknicken	We **had a picnic**. – Wir haben ein Picknick gemacht.
have a temperature	Fieber haben	
have got	haben	
have to	müssen	
Have you ever been to ...?	Warst du jemals/schon einmal in ...?	**Have you ever been to** Berlin? – Warst du schon einmal in Berlin?
haven't (= have not)	nicht haben	
he	er	
head	Kopf	
headache	Kopfschmerzen, Kopfweh	
healthy	gesund	
hear	hören	

hello	hallo	
help	helfen; Hilfe	
helpful	hilfreich, nützlich	
helpline	telefonischer Beratungsdienst; Notruf	
her	ihr(e, n); sie	
here	hier(her)	
here's (= here is)	hier ist	
hero	Held/in	1 **hero** – 2 **heroes**
hi	hallo, hi	
him	ihm, ihn	
hippo	Nilpferd	
hire	einstellen, beauftragen	
his	sein(e, r)	That is **his** pen. – Das ist sein Stift.
history	Geschichte	
hole	Loch	
holiday	Urlaub, Ferien	
holiday camp	Ferienlager	
home	zu Hause; nach Hause	
at home	zu Hause	
homework	Hausaufgaben	
hop off	schnell aussteigen	
hop on	schnell einsteigen	
hope	hoffen	
horoscope	Horoskop	I don't believe in **horoscopes**. – Ich glaube nicht an Horoskope.
hot	heiß	
hour	Stunde	
house	Haus	
how	wie	
How are things?	Wie geht's?	
How are you?	Wie geht es dir/Ihnen/euch?	
How old are you?	Wie alt bist du/seid ihr?	
hungry	hungrig	I am really **hungry**! – Ich habe richtig Hunger!
hurry up	sich beeilen	
hurt	wehtun, schmerzen	

I

I	ich	
I'd like (to)	ich würde gern ...	**I'd like** to fly to England. – Ich würde gern nach England fliegen.
I'll (= I will)	ich werde	
I'm (= I am)	ich bin, ich heiße	
ice cream	Eiscreme	
ICT (= information and communication technology)	Informatik	
idea	Idee	
if	wenn, falls	

ignore	ignorieren	
ill	krank	
important	wichtig	
in	in; auf	
Indian	indisch	I like **Indian** food. – Ich mag indisches Essen.
indoor	Hallen-	
insect	Insekt	
inside	drinnen; innen	
interested (in sth)	interessiert (an etw)	
interesting	interessant	
into	in	
invite	einladen	I'd like to **invite** you to my party. – Ich würde dich gern zu meiner Party einladen.
isn't (= is not)	ist nicht	
it	es	
it's (= it is)	es ist	
J		
jacket	Jacke	Don't forget your **jacket**! – Vergiss deine Jacke nicht!
January	Januar	
jelly bean	(bohnenförmiges) Geleebonbon	
join	mitmachen bei; beitreten	
juice	Saft	
jump	springen	
jungle	Dschungel, Urwald	
just	gleich; nur; einfach; gerade	
K		
keep	halten	
keeper	Wärter/in	
kid	Kind	
kind	Art, Sorte	
kind	nett, freundlich	
kitchen	Küche	
know	wissen; kennen	Do you **know** my sister? – Kennst du meine Schwester?
L		
label	beschriften	
lake	See	
large	groß	
last	letzte(r, s)	
late	(zu) spät	
be late	zu spät kommen	I **was late** to class. – Ich kam zu spät zum Unterricht.
later	später	
leaf/leaves	Blatt/Blätter	
learn	lernen	
leave	verlassen	

left	(nach) links	
on the/your left	links, auf der linken Seite	
leg	Bein	A horse has four **legs**. – Ein Pferd hat vier Beine.
lemonade	Limonade	
let	lassen	
let's (= let us)	lass(t) uns	
letter	Brief; Buchstabe	
library	Bibliothek, Bücherei	
life/lives	Leben	1 **life** – 2 **lives**
lighthouse	Leuchtturm	
lighthouse keeper	Leuchtturmwärter/in	
like	mögen	
like	wie	
like that	so; solche(r, s)	
like this	so	
line	Linie; Zeile	
lion	Löwe	
listen (to)	(zu)hören	
litter	Müll, Abfall	Put your **litter** in the bin. – Wirf deinen Müll in den Mülleimer.
little	wenig	
live	leben, wohnen	
living room	Wohnzimmer	
loads (of)	jede Menge, massenhaft	
logo	Abzeichen, Logo	
lonely	einsam	
long	lang	
look	sehen, schauen; aussehen	
look at	betrachten, sehen, anschauen	
look for	suchen (nach)	I am **looking for** my pen. – Ich suche meinen Stift.
look forward to	sich freuen auf	
look up	nachschlagen	
lots of	viel, jede Menge	
lottery	Lotterie	
loudly	laut	The man sings **loudly**. – Der Mann singt laut.
love	Liebe	
love	lieben; sehr gern mögen	
lovely	schön, hübsch	
be lucky	Glück haben	
lunch	Mittagessen	
lunchtime	Mittagszeit; Mittagspause	

M

made	Vergangenheitsform von „make“	She **made** tea. – Sie hat Tee gemacht.
make	machen	
make sb feel ...	jdm ein ... Gefühl geben	

man/men	Mann/Männer	
mane	Mähne	
many	viele	How **many** ...? – Wie viele ...?
map	(Land)karte	
March	März	
mark	markieren, kennzeichnen	
market	Markt	
marry	heiraten	
match	Spiel	
match (with)	zuordnen	**Match** the sentences. – Ordne die Sätze einander zu.
mate	Kumpel, Freund/in	
maths	Mathe	
may	können; dürfen	
maybe	vielleicht	
maze	Labyrinth, Irrgarten	
me	mir, mich; ich	
meal	Mahlzeit, Essen	
mealtime	Essenszeit	
mean	bedeuten; meinen	What does "ruler" **mean**? – Was bedeutet „ruler"?
meat	Fleisch	
mechanic	Mechaniker/in	
medicine	Medizin, Medikamente	
meet	(sich) treffen; kennenlernen	
mess	Unordnung, Durcheinander	
be a mess	chaotisch/unordentlich sein; ein einziges Durcheinander sein	
met	Vergangenheitsform von „meet"	I **met** my friends. – Ich habe meine Freunde getroffen.
mind	Geist, Verstand, Gedanken	
miniskirt	Minirock	
miss	verpassen; vermissen	
miss out	sich entgehen lassen	
missing	fehlend	
be missing	fehlen	
mix	(ver)mischen, anrühren	
mobile phone	Mobiltelefon, Handy	I can't find my **mobile phone**. – Ich kann mein Handy nicht finden.
Monday	Montag	
money	Geld	
month	Monat	
more	(noch) mehr	
in the morning	morgens, am Morgen, vormittags	
mother	Mutter	
Mother's Day	Muttertag	

mouse/mice	Maus/Mäuse	1 **mouse** – 2 **mice**
mouth	Mund	
Mr	Herr *(Anrede)*	
Mrs	Frau *(Anrede)*	
much	viel; sehr	
mum	Mama, Mutti	
music	Musik	I am listening to **music**. – Ich höre gerade Musik.
musician	Musiker/in	
muslim	Muslim/in; muslimisch	
must	müssen	
must not	nicht dürfen	
mustn't (= must not)	nicht dürfen	You **must not** run. – Du darfst nicht rennen.
my	mein(e)	

N

name	nennen	
nature	Natur	
need	brauchen	
need to	müssen	
never	niemals, nie	
new	neu	
New Year's Eve	Silvester	
news	Nachrichten	
next	dann; nächste(r, s)	**next** week – nächste Woche **next** month – nächsten Monat **next** year – nächstes Jahr
next to	neben	
nice	nett; schön	
night	Nacht	
no	nein; kein(e)	
north	Norden	
Northern Ireland	Nordirland	
not	nicht	
not yet	noch nicht	
notice	bemerken	
now	jetzt	Where are you **now**? – Wo bist du jetzt?
number	Zahl; Ziffer, Nummer; Aufgabe	
number	nummerieren	
nurse	(Kranken)schwester, (Kranken)pfleger	

O

(eight) o'clock	(acht) Uhr	
of	von; an	
of course	natürlich	
often	oft, häufig	I **often** read books. – Ich lese oft Bücher.
Oh dear!	Du meine Güte!	
oil	Öl	
old	alt	

olive oil	Olivenöl	
on	auf, an; in; am	My pen is **on** my desk. – Mein Stift ist auf meinem Schreibtisch.
on one's own	allein(e)	
onion	Zwiebel	
only	nur	
open	(sich) öffnen; aufmachen	
open	offen, geöffnet	
open up	sich öffnen	
opening times	Öffnungszeiten	
or	oder	
order	Ordnung, Reihenfolge	
other	andere(r, s)	
our	unser(e)	This is **our** dog, Lola. – Das ist unser Hund, Lola.
out	nach draußen, (he)raus	
outside	im Freien, draußen	
over	über	
P		
pack	packen	
packet	Packung, Schachtel	a **packet** of crisps – eine Packung Chips
page	Seite	
pair	Paar	
paper	Papier	
parents	Eltern	
park	parken	
part	Teil	
pasta	Nudeln	
paw	Pfote, Tatze	
pay	zahlen	
PE (= physical education)	(Sport)unterricht	
peel	schälen	**Peel** the onion. – Schäle die Zwiebel.
pen	Stift	
pencil	Bleistift	
pencil case	(Feder)mäppchen	
penguin	Pinguin	
people	Leute, Menschen	
pepper	Paprika; Pfeffer	
perfect	perfekt	
pet	Haustier	
phone	Telefon	
phone	anrufen	Let me **phone** my dad. – Lass mich meinen Papa anrufen.
phone call	(Telefon)anruf	
photo	Foto	
phrase	Ausdruck	
picnic	Picknick	
picture	Bild, Foto	That is a nice **picture**! – Das ist ein schönes Foto!
piece	Stück	

pink	rosa, pink	
place	Ort; Platz	
plan	planen	
plane	Flugzeug	
plant	Pflanze	
plastic	Plastik, Kunststoff	
play	Stück	
play	spielen	Do you **play** volleyball? – Spielst du Volleyball?
player	Spieler/in	
playground	Spielplatz	
playing	Spielen	
please	bitte	
p.m.	nachmittags, abends	8 **p.m.** – 8 Uhr abends / 20 Uhr
point (at)	zeigen/deuten (auf)	
police	Polizei	
police officer	Polizeibeamter/-beamtin	
polite	höflich	
poor	arm	
possible	möglich	
postcard	Postkarte	
pour	gießen, schütten	
practise	üben	
present	Geschenk	
present	präsentieren	
presentation	Präsentation	
pretty	hübsch	
pretty	ziemlich	
probably	wahrscheinlich	I will **probably** go to the cinema. – Ich werde wahrscheinlich ins Kino gehen.
professional	professionell, Profi-	
programme	Programm; Sendung	
protect	schützen	
put	setzen, legen, stellen; sortieren	
put away	wegräumen	
put in	hineintun	
put in order	in Ordnung bringen, ordnen	
put on	anziehen	

Q

queen	Königin	
question	Frage	
quickly	schnell	
quiet	leise, ruhig	She talks **quietly**. – Sie spricht leise.
quietly	leise; still	

R		
rainy	regnerisch	
reach	greifen; erreichen	
read	lesen	
read along	mitlesen	
reading	Lesen; Lesung	
ready	fertig, bereit	Are you **ready**? – Bist du bereit?
real	wirklich; echt	
really	wirklich	
recipe	Rezept	
record	aufnehmen	
red	rot	
relax	sich entspannen	
repair	reparieren	
repeat	wiederholen	**Repeat** the words. – Wiederhole die Wörter.
report	berichten	
respect	Respekt, Achtung	
rich	reich	
ride	Fahrt; Tour	
right	(nach) rechts; richtig	
right here	genau hier	
be right	Recht haben	
on the/your right	rechts, auf der rechten Seite	The cinema is **on the right**. – Das Kino liegt auf der rechten Seite.
river	Fluss	
River Main	Main	
role play	Rollenspiel	
Rome	Rom	**Rome** is the capital of Italy. – Rom ist die Hauptstadt von Italien.
room	Zimmer	
root	Wurzel	
route	Route, Strecke	
row	rudern	
rubber	Radiergummi	
rubbish	Müll	
rule	Regel	
ruler	Lineal	
run	laufen, rennen	
run around	herumrennen	

S		
sad	traurig	
sadly	traurig; betrübt	
safely	sicher	
salad	Salat	I am making a **salad**. – Ich mache gerade einen Salat.
salt	Salz	
salt water	Salzwasser	
salted	gesalzen	
the same	der-/die-/dasselbe; gleich	

sandcastle	Sandburg	
sari	Sari (gewickeltes Gewand indischer Frauen)	
sat	Vergangenheitsform von „sit“	He **sat** under a tree. – Er saß unter einem Baum.
Saturday	Samstag	
sausage	Wurst, Würstchen	
save	retten	
saw	Vergangenheitsform von „see“	I **saw** the tigers. – Ich sah die Tiger.
say	sagen	
school	Schule	
school building	Schulgebäude	
school grounds	Schulgelände	
school uniform	Schuluniform	
schoolbag	Schultasche	
science	(Natur)wissenschaft	
(pair of) scissors	Schere	Can you give me the **scissors**, please? – Kannst du mir bitte die Schere geben?
score a goal	ein Tor schießen	
Scotland	Schottland	
screen	Leinwand; Bildschirm	
the sea	Meer, See	
seat	Sitzplatz, Platz	
see	sehen	
see you	bis dann, bis bald	
seen	siehe „see“	I have **seen** a monster. – Ich habe ein Monster gesehen.
sell	verkaufen	
send	(zu)schicken	
sentence	Satz	
sentence part	Satzteil	
series	Serie, Reihe	
set off	(an)zünden	
she	sie	
shipwreck	Schiffswrack, Schiffbruch	
shirt	Hemd; Bluse	
shoe	Schuh	
shop	Geschäft, Laden	
shop	einkaufen	
shop assistant	Verkäufer/in	The **shop assistant** works in a shop. – Der Verkäufer arbeitet in einem Laden.
shopping tour	Einkaufsbummel	
short	kurz	
short form	Abkürzung	
should	sollte/müsste	
show	zeigen	
sight	Sehenswürdigkeit	
sightseeing tour	Rundfahrt	
sing	singen	
sing along	mitsingen	

sister	Schwester	
sit	sitzen	
sketchbook	Skizzenbuch	
skirt	Rock	She is wearing a blue **skirt**. – Sie trägt einen blauen Rock.
sky	Himmel	
skyscraper	Wolkenkratzer	
sleep	schlafen	
sleep over	über Nacht bleiben, übernachten	
small	klein	
smell (of)	riechen (nach)	
smoking	Rauchen	
snake	Schlange	I don't like **snakes**. – Ich mag keine Schlangen.
snowy	schneereich; verschneit	
so	so; deshalb; also	
soap (opera)	Seifenoper, Soap	
sock	Socke	
some	einige; etwas	
someone	jemand	
something	etwas	
something else	(noch) etwas anderes	
sometimes	manchmal	
soon	bald	
sore	wund, entzündet	
sore throat	Halsschmerzen	I have a **sore throat**. – Ich habe Halsschmerzen.
sorry	Entschuldigung!	
I'm sorry.	Das tut mir leid.	
sort	sortieren	
sound	Geräusch, Klang; Ton	
sound	klingen, sich anhören	
soup	Suppe	
Spain	Spanien	
speech bubble	Sprechblase	
spend	ausgeben (*Geld*); verbringen (*Zeit*)	
spoon	Löffel	
sports	Sport; Sportart	
sports club	Sportverein	
sports kit	Sportkleidung, Sportsachen	I need my **sports kit** for PE. – Ich brauche meine Sportsachen für den Sportunterricht.
sports programme	Sportsendung	
spot	Fleck; Stelle	
stadium	Stadion	
stall	(Verkaufs)stand	
stand	stehen	
start	Anfang, Beginn	
start	anfangen, beginnen	
stay	bleiben; wohnen	

step	treten	
still	immer noch	
stop	aufhören; beenden	Please **stop** singing! – Bitte hör auf zu singen!
Stop it!	Hör auf (damit)!, Hört auf (damit)!	
storm	Sturm	
story	Geschichte, Erzählung	
straight (on)	gerade(aus)	
street	Straße	
stripe	Streifen	
strong	stark	
student	Schüler/in	
style	frisieren	
subject	Schulfach	My favourite **subject** is maths. – Mein Lieblingsfach ist Mathe.
summer	Sommer	
sun	Sonne	
sun cream	Sonnencreme	
Sunday	Sonntag	
sunglasses	Sonnenbrille	
sunny	sonnig	
sure	sicher	
surprise	Überraschung	
surprise party	Überraschungsparty	
survivor	Überlebende/r	
sweet	süß	
sweets	Süßigkeiten	
swim	schwimmen	
swimming	Schwimmen	Let's go **swimming**! – Lasst uns schwimmen gehen!
swimming course	Schwimmkurs	
swimming pool	Schwimmbecken, -bad	
swimwear	Badebekleidung	

T

T. Rex (= tyrannosaurus rex)	Tyrannosaurus Rex	
table	Tabelle; Tisch	
tail	Schwanz	
take	(mit)nehmen; machen; wegnehmen, stehlen	
take a photo	ein Foto machen	
take a tour	eine Tour/Führung machen	
take care of	sich kümmern um, versorgen	My mum **takes care** of me. – Meine Mama kümmert sich um mich.
take notes	(sich) Notizen machen	
take out	hinausbringen	
take part (in)	teilnehmen (an)	
take place	stattfinden	

taken	siehe „take“	He has **taken** his medicine. – Er hat seine Medikamente genommen.
talent show	Talentwettbewerb	
talk	Gespräch; Unterhaltung	
talk (to)	sprechen/reden/sich unterhalten (mit)	
tall	hoch; groß	
target task	Zielaufgabe	
tea	Tee	
teacher	Lehrer/in	
tell	erzählen; sagen	
temperature	Temperatur; Fieber	
terrible	schrecklich, furchtbar	
text	eine SMS/Kurznachricht schicken	I'll **text** Jasmine later. – Ich schicke Jasmine nachher eine SMS.
text message	SMS, Kurznachricht	
text messaging	Versenden von SMS/ Kurznachrichten	
than	als	She is taller **than** him. – Sie ist größer als er.
thank you	danke	
that	dass; das; der/die/das	
that's (= that is)	das ist	
the	der/die/das	
their	ihr, ihre	
them	sie, ihnen	
theme	Thema; Lektion, Kapitel	
then	dann, danach	
there	dort, da; dorthin, dahin	
there are	da sind; es gibt	
there is	da ist; es gibt	**There is** a book on my desk. – Auf meinem Schreibtisch ist ein Buch.
there's (= there is)	da ist; es gibt	
these	diese	
they	sie	
thing	Ding, Gegenstand, Sache	
think	denken, glauben, meinen	
think of	denken an; sich ausdenken	
this	diese(r, s); das	
those	diese; jene	
threatening	Droh-; bedrohlich	
throat	Rachen, Hals	
through	durch	
tick	abhaken, ankreuzen	
tidied	siehe „tidy“	He has **tidied** his room. – Er hat sein Zimmer aufgeräumt.
tidy	aufräumen	
tie	Krawatte	
time	Uhrzeit, Zeit; Mal	
tip	Tipp	
tired	müde	

title	Titel	
to	in, nach, zu, an; bis; um zu; mit; für; bei	
today	heute	
together	zusammen, gemeinsam	
tomato/tomatoes	Tomate/Tomaten	1 **tomato** – 2 **tomatoes**
tomorrow	morgen	
too	zu; auch	
took	Vergangenheitsform von „take“	I **took** a photo. – Ich habe ein Foto gemacht.
tooth/teeth	Zahn/Zähne	
toothbrush	Zahnbürste	
top	Spitze; Top-	
torch	Taschenlampe, Fackel	
tortoise	(Land)schildkröte	
tour guide	Reiseführer/in, Reiseleiter/in	
tower	Turm	
traditional	traditionell	
train	Zug, Eisenbahn	
trainer	Turnschuh	Where are my **trainers**? – Wo sind meine Turnschuhe?
treasure hunt	Schatzsuche; Schnitzeljagd	
tree	Baum	
Trick or treat!	Süßes oder Saures!	
trip	Ausflug; Reise, Fahrt	
trip over	fallen über; stolpern über	
trouble	Schwierigkeiten; schwierige Lebenssituation	
trousers	Hose	
trust	vertrauen	
the Tube	(Londoner) U-Bahn	
Turkey	Türkei	
turn	sich drehen; abbiegen	
turn on	einschalten	
TV (= television)	Fernseher; Fernsehen	Let’s turn on the **TV**. – Lasst uns den Fernseher einschalten.
TV programme	Fernsehsendung	

U

ugh	bäh, igitt	
UK (= United Kingdom)	das Vereinigte Königreich	
under	unter	
underground	U-Bahn	
underline	unterstreichen	
underwater	Unterwasser-	
unscramble	sortieren, wieder ordnen	

untidy	unordentlich, ungepflegt	
up to	bis (zu)	
us	uns	
USA (= United States of America)	USA, Vereinigte Staaten von Amerika	Have you ever been to the **USA**? – Warst du schon einmal in den USA?
use	benutzen	
using	Nutzen	
usually	gewöhnlich, normalerweise	

V

Valentine's Day	Valentinstag	
vegetable	Gemüse	
vegetable stick	Gemüsestick	
very	sehr	
vet (= veterinarian)	Tierarzt/-ärztin	
video game	Videospiel	
video game designer	Videospielentwickler/in	
view	Ausblick, Aussicht	
vinegar	Essig	I don't like **chips** with vinegar. – Ich mag keine Pommes mit Essig.
visit	Besuch	
visit	besuchen	
voucher	Gutschein	

W

sb cannot wait (to do sth)	jmd kann es kaum erwarten (, etw zu tun)	
walk	gehen, laufen	
want	wollen	
want sb to do sth	wollen, dass jmd etw tut	
was	Vergangenheitsform von „be“	I **was** tired. – Ich war müde.
watch	beobachten; anschauen	
watch TV	fernsehen	
watching	Beobachten, Anschauen	
watching TV	Fernsehen	
water	Wasser	
wave	Welle	I **will** – ich werde you **will** – du wirst he/she/it **will** – er/sie/es wird we **will** – wir werden you **will** – ihr werdet they **will** – sie werden
way	Weg; Art, Weise	
way out	Ausgang	
we	wir	
we'll (= we will)	wir werden	
we're (= we are)	wir sind	
we've (= we have)	wir haben	
wear	tragen	
weather	Wetter	
Wednesday	Mittwoch	
week	Woche	

weekend	Wochenende	
at the weekend	am Wochenende	
welcome (to)	willkommen (in)	
well	gut	
well	nun, nun ja, tja	
went	Vergangenheitsform von „go"	I **went** to the beach. – Ich bin zum Strand gegangen.
were	Vergangenheitsform von „be"	We **were** happy. – Wir waren glücklich.
whale	Wal	
what	was; welche(r, s)	
What about ...?	Was ist mit ...?, Wie wäre es mit ...?	
What is it about?	Worum geht es?	
what's (= what is)	was ist; wie lautet	
What's ... like?	Wie ist ...?	**What's** Scotland **like**? – Wie ist Schottland?
what's more	außerdem	
What's on?	Was ist los?, Was steht an?	
What's wrong?	Was ist los?	
What's your name?	Wie heißt du?, Wie heißen Sie?	
wheel	Rad	
wheelchair	Rollstuhl	
when	wenn; als; wann	
where	wo, wohin	
Where are you from?	Wo kommst du her?	
which	welche(r, s); der/die/das	
who	wer; der/die/das	**Who** are you? – Wer bist du?
why	warum	
will	werden	
win	gewinnen	
window	Fenster	
windy	windig	
wish	Wunsch	
with	mit; zu	
woman/women	Frau/Frauen	1 **woman** – 2 **women**
won't	nicht werden	
wonderful	wunderbar, wundervoll	
word	Wort	
word field	Wortfeld	
wordsearch	Wortsuchrätsel	
work	arbeiten; funktionieren	
world	Welt, Erde	
worried	beunruhigt, besorgt	
worriedly	beunruhigt, besorgt	
worst	schlechteste(r, s), schlimmste(r, s)	

would	würde(st, n, t)	
would like (to)	möchte (gern)	I **would like to** listen to music. – Ich würde gern Musik hören.
wouldn't (= would not)	würde(st, n, t) nicht	
write	schreiben	
write down	aufschreiben	
wrong	falsch	

Y

yeah	ja	
year	Jahr	
yellow	gelb	
yes	ja	
yesterday	gestern	What did you do **yesterday**? – Was hast du gestern gemacht?
you	du, dich, dir, Sie, Ihnen; ihr, euch	
you're (= you are)	du bist; ihr seid	
You're welcome.	Gern geschehen., Bitte.	
young	jung	
younger	jünger	
your	dein(e); euer/eure; Ihr(e)	
youth club	Jugendzentrum	

The days of the week

Monday
Tuesday
Wednesday
Thursday
Friday
Saturday
Sunday

The months

January	July
February	August
March	September
April	October
May	November
June	December

Numbers

0	zero
1	one
2	two
3	three
4	four
5	five
6	six
7	seven
8	eight
9	nine

10	ten
11	eleven
12	twelve
13	thirteen
14	fourteen
15	fifteen
16	sixteen
17	seventeen
18	eighteen
19	nineteen

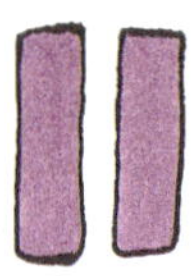

20	twenty
21	twenty-one
22	twenty-two
23	twenty-three
24	twenty-four
25	twenty-five
26	twenty-six
27	twenty-seven
28	twenty-eight
29	twenty-nine

30	thirty
31	thirty-one

40	forty
50	fifty
60	sixty
70	seventy
80	eighty
90	ninety
100	one hundred

1st	first
2nd	second
3rd	third
4th	fourth
5th	fifth
6th	sixth
7th	seventh
8th	eighth
9th	ninth
10th	tenth
11th	eleventh
12th	twelfth
13th	thirteenth
14th	fourteenth
15th	fifteenth
16th	sixteenth
17th	seventeenth
18th	eighteenth
19th	nineteenth
20th	twentieth
21st	twenty-first
22nd	twenty-second
...	
30th	thirtieth
31st	thirty-first

Trackliste

Alle Audiodateien findest du unter:

www.westermann.de/webcode

Gib den folgenden Webcode ein:

WES-149122-001

Dann kannst du die Dateien herunterladen.

Theme 1: After the holidays

Holidays

1. 1 Megan's holiday
2. 3 Back home
3. 4 Weather words
4. 9 I didn't
5. 11 Lynn's holiday diary

Back to school

6. 1 Back to school
7. 6 School sounds
8. 10 A new classmate

Theme 2: Around London

Famous sights

9. 2 Famous sights
10. 9 Your favourite sights
11. 12 A sightseeing tour

London Zoo

12. 1 Two pictures
13. 2 What happened?
14. 3a The way to London Zoo
15. 3c The way to London Zoo
16. 4 Giving directions
17. 5 Together again
18. 8 Lions
19. 9 Which animal is it?
20. 11 A day out

Theme 3: Dreams

The future

21. 1 Kitchen talk
22. 3 Talking on the phone
23. 10 Jobs

Heroes

24. 1 All kinds of heroes
25. 4 Grace Darling
26. 5 What are the words?
27. 8 A dramatic reading

Theme 4: Celebrations

Festivals

28. 1b Lots of festivals
29. 1d Lots of festivals
30. 4 Sound check
31. 5 It's Diwali time

Birthdays

32. 1 A brilliant idea
33. 2 Let's get started
34. 3 What do they want to buy?
35. 4 What's in the party box?
36. 8 Looking for a present
37. 18 The surprise party

Theme 5: Dos and don'ts

Rules at home

38. 1 Problems
39. 2 Megan and her mum
40. 3 Talking to Dad
41. 4 A chat

Rules at school

42. 1 Haverstock school rules
43. 10 What is happening?

Theme 6: Let's go!

What's on?

44. 2 A weekend in Camden
45. 3 Visiting a friend
46. 7 At the doctor's
47. 8 What's the problem?

Holiday plans

48. 1 Have you ever ...?
49. 2 Choose an activity
50. 3 Holiday plans
51. 9 On the beach in Cornwall
52. 10 A holiday dialogue

Audiodateien

Tonstudio: TEFL AUDIO, London; Produzent: John Green, Ton: Tim Woolf; dbmedia.de, Neuwied; Produzent: Stephan Dupré

Gesprochen von: Roger May; Jenny Bryce; Brian Bowles; Harriet Kershaw; John Hasler; Raphael von Blumenthal; Rachael Miller sowie Phil Lewis; Steve England; Pete Cousin; Margaret Ashley; Scott Tunnix; Juliet Prew; Karina Moore; Sonny Crowe; Priya Alexander; Gil Thom; Gracie Beresford; Ethan Sefton; Jake Sefton; Sonny Crowe; Oliver Bonallack; Elliott Brand; Lola Watts; Tomi North; Sam North; Sofia Brown; Lily Bridge; Zac Ciscon; Mia Ciscon

Songs: 4 – I didn't © Bildungshaus Schulbuchverlage GmbH, Braunschweig. Music Tim Woolf, London.
48 – Have you ever? © Westermann Bildungsmedien Verlag GmbH, Braunschweig. Music Tobias Friedrich, Berlin.

Bildquellen

|Alamy Stock Photo, Abingdon/Oxfordshire: Armstead, Johnny 28.1; Bollo, Carlo 96.1; imageBROKER 93.2; Londonstills.com 22.2; R Handley, Richard 43.1; Sherratt, Adrian 81.3; WENN Rights Ltd 25.3. |Alamy Stock Photo (RMB), Abingdon/Oxfordshire: 92.1; Alex Segre 28.3; imageBROKER/Cuveland, Justus de 34.8; Michael Cullen 92.7; Steve Vidler 16.2; True Images 81.2; © KAKIMAGE 57.2. |ddp images GmbH, Hamburg: Lennart Preiss 92.3. |Diekmann, Udo, Berlin: 25.4. |fotolia.com, New York: bertys30 34.10; Geijer, K. 34.9; JiSign 101.1, 101.2, 101.3, 101.4; Monkey Business 57.3; moonrun 5.2, 10.1, 16.1, 26.1, 57.1, 81.1, 93.1; OHRAUGE 23.3; robcartorres 34.4; Smileus 54.5. |Getty Images, München: FatCamera 55.1; Kitwood, Dan 25.1, 28.4. |Getty Images (RF), München: Leland Bobbe 55.2. |Hamill, Aisling, Braunschweig: 82.2. |Interfoto, München: Travel Library / Grant Pritchard 55.4. |iStockphoto.com, Calgary: 60.1; 25ehaag6 34.3; _ultraforma_ 26.4; AndreyKrav 25.2; arsenisspyros 54.1; AYImages 34.11; claudiodivizia 26.5; dolgachov 56.1; JoshuaMade 28.5; littleny 26.3; mammuth 22.1; MATJAZ SLANIC 92.4; monkeybusinessimages Titel; santypan 54.4; Spondylolithesis 37.1; svetikd 55.3; Vitalii Hulai 34.6. |Klahold, Doreen, Braunschweig: 64.1, 64.2, 64.3, 64.4, 64.5, 64.6. |Krause, Charlotte, Wolfenbüttel: 82.1, 82.3, 82.4, 82.5, 82.6, 82.7, 82.8. |mauritius images GmbH, Mittenwald: Alamy / Schneider, Daniele / Photononstop 54.3. |Mohm, Julia, Braunschweig: 17.1, 17.2, 17.3, 17.4, 19.1. |Picture-Alliance GmbH, Frankfurt/M.: dpa / ABC Television Network 92.8; dpa/Karl-Josef Hildenbrand 54.2. |Schmidt-Brücken, Frank, Weiterstadt: 26.2, 26.6. |Schumann, Friederike, Berlin: 37.2. |Shutterstock.com, New York: Anamwong, Sira 94.1; Anton_Ivanov 25.5; Artgraphixel 94.3; ChameleonsEye 23.4; Fotogroove 94.5; FrameStockFootages 43.6; GUDKOV ANDREY 34.1; Ian_Stewart 43.5; konstantinks 94.4; Luchenko, Yana 94.2; Sergei Mironenko 34.5; Smileus 34.2. |Shutterstock.com (RM), New York: Warner Bros/Kobal 92.5. |stock.adobe.com, Dublin: AA+W 28.6; Aufort, Jérome 34.7; bayu harsa 22.3; Cervo, Diego 43.3; Chan, Richie 28.2; denisgorelkin 73.1, 73.2, 73.3, 73.4; f11photo 29.1; fedorovekb 92.2; giemmephoto 23.2; JackF 43.4; Kadmy 43.2; Maridav 23.1; motortion 92.6; romaset 43.7; van Wijk, Fred 26.7; WavebreakMediaMicro 43.8; YUN_1 34.12. |Wilson, Emily, Berkshire: 14.1. |Zwick, Joachim, Gießen: 5.1.

Wir arbeiten sehr sorgfältig daran, für alle verwendeten Abbildungen die Rechteinhaberinnen und Rechteinhaber zu ermitteln. Sollte uns dies im Einzelfall nicht vollständig gelungen sein, werden berechtigte Ansprüche selbstverständlich im Rahmen der üblichen Vereinbarungen abgegolten.